Betrayed by his brothers and cut down in his youth, Sudika-mbambi dropped through the bottom of his grave, and in the red of twilight before the sky went dark, he met an old woman, half black and half white, at the side of a river.

"You who must find the path through the land of ghosts," said the Grandmother, "carry close to your body this calabash of red pepper and this calabash of wisdom."

Bantu folktale

This book is dedicated to my grandchildren: Sarah Ann Metzger who runs with the wolves and her sister Jamie Lynn who showed me Grandmother Willow in the blooming lilac.

Con los pobres de la tierra nuestra suerte echamos.

Dedicated also to Ernestine Hemmings and the budding poets of Crenshaw High who bear the seeds of the future.

MICHAEL ORTIZ HILL

THE VILLAGE OF THE WATER SPIRITS

The Dreams of African Americans

with

Mandaza Augustine Kandemwa

SPRING PUBLICATIONS, INC.
PUTNAM, CONNECTICUT

Copyright © 2006 by Spring Publications, Inc.

Published by Spring Publications, Inc.
Putnam, Conn.
www.springpublications.com

Inquiries should be addressed to:
PO Box 230212
New York, N.Y. 10023
editor@springpublications.com

Distributed by The Continuum International Publishing Group
80 Maiden Lane, Suite 704
New York, N.Y. 10038
Tel: 212 953 5858
Fax: 212 953 5944
www.continuumbooks.com

First Edition 2006

Printed in Canada

Design: white.room productions, New York

Cover image: Cave at Siloswane where the old spirits of the Bushman people
were summoned (Photo: David Steinberg)

Library of Congress Cataloging-in-Publication Data

Hill, Michael Ortiz.
    The village of the water spirits : the dreams of African Americans / Michael Ortiz Hill; with
Mandaza Augustine Kandemwa. — 1st ed.
        p. cm.
    Includes bibliographical references.
    ISBN-13: 978-0-88214-553-2 (pbk. : alk. paper)
    ISBN-10: 0-88214-553-3 (pbk. : alk. paper)
    1. African Americans–Psychology. 2. African Americans–Medicine. 3. African Americans —
Religion. 4. Traditional medicine — Africa. 5. Dream interpretation–Africa. I. Kandemwa,
Mandaza Augustine. II. Title.

E185.625.H56 2006
155.8'496073 — dc22

                                                                    2006033683

∞ The paper used in this publication meets the minimum requirements of
the American National Standard for Information Sciences — Permanence of
Paper for Printed Library Materials,
ANSI Z39.48-1992.

CONTENTS

PREFACE

Michael Ortiz Hill is a scholar-initiate of Africana wisdom traditions. He belongs to a new intellectual movement that is emerging to capture the indigenous meanings of
Africana cultures and make them as strong and creative as possible. This new movement is constantly stewarding, arbitrating,
and rethinking the indigenous values, principles, and meth-
odologies of Africana cultures. The best thinkers of this new
movement are staging an intellectual revolution that is moving
the exploration of Africana wisdom traditions from the mar-
gins to the center of modernity around the world. In this book,
THE VILLAGE OF WATER SPIRITS, Michael deals with the enduring legacy of wisdom among African American people and explores the religious world that they built in the North American
Diaspora for the last three centuries. This work is based on two
sources. First, it relies on long conversations between Michael
and the Shona nganga (medicine man) Mandaza Kandemwa.
These conversations deal with what they perceive as the spirit
world of African Americans as revealed in their dreams. In addition, this book is based on Michael's scholarly research into
the African shape of the African-American soul.

This work has two dimensions: a deconstructive dimension
and a creative dimension. The deconstructive dimension ex-
amines critically the phenomenon that Valentin Mudimbe has
called the "Colonial Library," which he sees as the set of rep-
resentations and texts that have collectively "invented" Africa

as a locus of difference and alterity. In his seminal work THE INVENTION OF AFRICA, Mudimbe does a good job of exposing how an African episteme was a product of a complex interplay of different forms of Western power — political and cognitive — that created the Colonial Library, the objectifying ordered caricature of African socio-cultural realities (to use Wim van Binsbergen's words). Michael exposes the effects of the Colonial Library against the descendants of enslaved Africans in North America. He shows how Western ethnocentrism and racism are still alive, but he emphasizes the way the counter-hegemonic spirit has enabled African Americans to resist the dehumanizing effects of the Colonial Library. He supports his ideas with dreams that African Americans have about white people to underscore the spiritual nature of resistance to the Colonial Library in North America.

The creative dimension of Michael's work enables us to appreciate the innovative approaches that African Americans used to maintain their African cosmological orientation. Michael makes two main claims. First, he argues that African Americans built religious worlds that enabled them to develop various responses and modes of resistance to the alienating process of slavery and modernity. He focuses on the concept of initiation, which he sees as a cornerstone of African American religious worlds. Initiation means different things to different people. For Michael, the concept of initiation in the African religious worlds has to deal with the fact of yielding to Spirit. He attempts to show how rites of initiation in African American religious worlds are still rooted in their African understandings and the ordeal of the Middle Passage.

The second claim and the most important that Michael makes is that water spirits play a central role in African American cosmological orientation. He starts by explaining water spirits as the most powerful of all the spirits, who come out of the body of God, and return to it. He describes the religious function that they fulfill in the name of the Ultimate

Creator. Then, Michael shows the importance of water spirits in the African worlds from which African Americans originated. He focuses on the traditions of the water spirits in those parts of Central Africa — especially the coastal Bantu people who supplied so many slaves to the Americas. Joining hands with Mandaza, they attempt to explain how the spiritual understandings deriving from the water spirits have endured among African Americans.

THE VILLAGE OF WATER SPIRITS is a testament to the enduring legacy of wisdom in the African American culture. It stands as a contribution to the archeology of discourses by scholar-initiates who assert that African modes of thought and being are still alive in the orientations of African Americans. It explores the intimate aspects of life of African Americans and shows how they have built worlds of meaning to resist the dehumanizing Western slavery and racism. After reading this work, one cannot help but realize how true are the insights of the following Akan proverb: "If you visit a place and hear their children singing songs, these songs are the very ones sung by their ancestors and handed down to them."

Dr. Kykosa Kajangu
Department of Religion and Philosophy,
Southwestern University

INTRODUCTION

It was a hot August night in the early nineties when I first caught a glimpse of the arcane and thoroughly African patterns in the dream life of a Mr. Cary, a fifty-two-year-old African American then incarcerated in a prison in upstate New York. Straight out of Pittsburgh via the Bronx, Mr. Cary had been keeping journals of his dreams for years. His grandmother had taught him to pay attention to his dreams when he was a boy, and he had noted that some of them foretold the future.

"One of the high points of being in jail," he wrote me, "is you get to sleep and dream a lot. One thing the white man's system can't take away from me are my nightly dreams."

I had received Mr. Cary's dreams just a few months after I'd begun researching the patterns in white and black people's dreams about each other. I had dug into the scholarship on the African worlds that black Americans came out of, but it never dawned on me that those worlds could conceivably be entirely intact in their nightly dreams. Indeed, I would have regarded the idea as fairly preposterous: Few African-Americans I knew felt any essential tie to the Motherland. That long night I was riven with astonishment and perplexity as I shuffled between dreams and sheathes of xeroxed manuscripts on Bantu culture, and although I could not grasp the implications, it was irrefutable that Mr. Cary was dreaming whites in exactly the same fashion that Bantu people have understood whiteness since the Portuguese first made contact with the kingdom of the Kongo

in the fifteenth century. In other words, Africa has kept faith
with the African-American soul. In spite of the bitter historical
realities of separation upon separation upon separation, black
culture in America is an undeniably African culture even, if not
especially, in the intimate matters of the heart.

It soon became clear that I had to seek out a Bantu medicine
man to interpret the over one hundred dreams I had collected.
Moreover, God willing, I needed to be initiated into the Bantu
spirit world because as an author I wanted to do justice to
the strange discovery of the subterranean connection between
Africa and America. How else could I genuinely know the true
meaning of the book I was apparently being asked to write?
By a rather mysterious route that I recount in a companion
book, TWIN OF ANOTHER TRIBE (the forthcoming new edition
of GATHERING IN THE NAMES), I was led to a remarkable and
tender friendship with Mandaza Augustine Kandemwa, who initiated me into the healing tradition of the Shona and Ndebele
people of Zimbabwe. This book is based on our long conversations about the spirit world of black Americans as revealed in
their dreams and on my research into the African shape of the
African-American soul.

I believe Mandaza to be the perfect interpreter of these
dreams for several reasons. His ritual tradition, the ngoma of the
water spirits, played, as we shall see, a very direct role in what
became African-American culture, and not a few of the dreams
I presented him he recognized as "water spirit" dreams. More
than any other Bantu healer I've met, Mandaza's day-to-day work
curing and initiating people is involved with dream-telling and
interpretation, and his own spiritual life has been completely
formed from the realm of dreaming. As a Shona tribesman, his
people are of the Zambezi circle," that cultural province spreading east and south from coastal Angola and Zaire that was so
viciously exploited by the trans-Atlantic slave trade, and one occasionally hears stories of the trade in Zimbabwean villages.
Finally, Mandaza is a child of apartheid and knows intimately in

himself and among his kin and patients the spiritual dilemmas of being black in a world controlled by whites. The fierce kindness and uncompromised intelligence with which he held the dreams of African-Americans is evident in his words.

As a biracial Mexican/Anglo man who has labored in the morass of racial politics in America all of my life, it is a great pleasure to offer this gift from Africa. When I was a young man, I cast my lot with the black militants during those bleak days in the late seventies when our ideas thickened with the passions of suicide and criminality

It's been, mercifully, a long time since I yearned to spill blood for a just cause, but when I began working on this book, I found myself haunted by my past, every thought and written word scrutinized by the spirit of Malcolm X, George Jackson and Huey P. Newton. An honorable lot, yes, but they completely paralyzed my efforts to break out and find something new to say about race in America. I returned instead to my old mentor, James Baldwin — his excruciating compassion and his refusal to lie. His spirit stayed close to me through some damned difficult passages.

The gift that Mandaza and I offer over to the reader in its deepest meaning is the unbroken circle between Africa and America. I begin and end THE VILLAGE OF THE WATER SPIRITS invoking this circle because for us the story is now complete.

> I wus baptised in the Tangipaho River right here in Osyka, an' all de folks wus shoutin' an' I went down in de water shoutin' — I tell yo' I neber wus so happy as I wus dat day, an' I is been a good Christian woman eber since I wus baptised. I talks to de Lord an' his spirit tells me I is livin' right. I aint got many days to live but I am gwine to meet my Maker shoutin' — He tells us to shout fur joy.

If you ask me about healing. I have to talk about
the water spirits because they are the ones that heal.
I do not. I am their servant.

Mandaza Kandemwa

WATERMARKS

1

TRACES OF A FLOWING SECRET

Although Mandaza and I affectionately call each other "mapatya," twin brother, I am in no way his equal when it comes to stamina. The long weeks of being initiated by him and the rigor of working alongside him as his apprentice as we initiated a small group of people had completely exhausted me. Mandaza as usual appeared inexhaustible and in generous good humor when we sat down on the cement floor of the house of his spirits and I cracked open my notebook with over a hundred dreams of African-Americans about white people. Passing the sacred snuff between us as I turned on the tape recorder, he said, "Dreams are a language I understand." I knew this to be true, for Mandaza is a healer and dreamteller, a nganga in the living spiritual tradition that is at the headwaters of what eventually became African-American culture.

What do I mean by "headwaters"? When you follow a river upstream, you eventually come to its source. A few months after Los Angeles burned when a few white policemen were exonerated in the beating of a black motorist, Rodney King, I was quite lost in researching white people's dreams about blacks and black people's dreams about whites. I was compelled to offer the dreams of black Americans to a medicine man who would understand their deepest meanings. In ways I will never understand, I was led directly to Mandaza. My own dreams became the river of images I followed upstream. I had dreamt of

Mandaza twice in the nine years before I met him: the words he would greet me with, a dance I would watch him do on the banks of the Zambezi. He and his wife Simakuhle also dreamt of me in anticipation of my arrival. After we had settled into our recognition of each other during my first initiation, which is to say after the three of us puzzled out the meaning of the dreams that brought us together, Mandaza laughed: tender, appreciative and astonished. "That is how these spirits work," he said.

Headwaters. Again, what do I mean by headwaters? When one follows the meandering path of the river downstream, it eventually passes through various villages. African-American culture is as complex and multiple as any culture on the planet – cultures within cultures within cultures, not to mention the particular struggles of any given soul, any given family. And yet, Mandaza sees in their dreams that the various worlds of black Americans are fed by the same river, a river he returns to again and again to meet his ancestors.

Judith Gleason recalls a conversation with a water spirit priest whose family for centuries had guarded and passed on the secrets of the Niger River. She expressed her concern that perhaps the presence of foreign film makers was violating the sanctity of the rites when the spirits are called down to dance through the bodies of the initiates.

"All along the river," he said, "from sources to sea, religion – Islam, Christianity – will never be able to destroy tradition. All people who live near the water defend it. Contact with water by its very nature safeguards the primordial secrets."

Furthermore, he explained that the "dancers traced certain concepts of cosmic organization on the sand with their feet without explanation ever having been given to them. Highly initiated elders were even able to read invisible points in the dancers' patterns – spaces representing spiritual beings too ancient and august to possess human beings and be danced by them. To perform such dances before the camera, therefore, would be in no way to disclose their meaning, to which even dancers themselves were after not privy."

"The patterns," continues Gleason, "replicate the beginning of things." She came to think of them as watermarks, "traces of a flowing secret."

As Mandaza's apprentice, I want to offer an echo chamber so that his words fully resonate for people on this side of the Atlantic. I beg the readers' indulgence that, at least in these first three chapters, I sketch out from the angle of a researcher how any of the statements I will make alongside my twin could possibly be true. I am well aware that they go against the grain of what is regarded as "common sense" in America.

Early on in our friendship, Mandaza and I refreshed ourselves at the local Wimpy's Burgers at Victoria Falls. I struggled to remember nightmares that had been given to me by my daughter's teenage friend Nikki — quintessentially young, gifted, and black and working very hard to make sense of America.

"Those blacks you talk about," Mandaza said, "many of them are children of the water spirits."

"What makes you say that?" I asked.

"They suffer so much for the sake of the world," was his simple response.

Mandaza's words reminded me of what Melville Herskovits had written back in 1941 about the strong influence that priests of the water spirits had on the formation of African-American culture. Herskovits was the first scholar to see that the primary ritual of black Baptist culture in America, full immersion baptism, was African in origin. Herskovits notes that ". . . the intransigence of the priests of the river cult was so marked that, more than any other group of holy men, they were sold into slavery to rid the conquerors of troublesome leaders. In all those parts of the New World where African religious beliefs have persisted, moreover, the river cult or in broader terms, the cult of water spirits, holds an important place. All this testifies to the vitality of this element in African religion and supports the conclusion to be drawn from the hint in the Dahomean data as to the possible influence such priests wielded even as slaves."

Dominique Zahan has pointed out that water is the central religious motif in black Africa. Cross-culturally and across the range of wet and dry geographies, rivers, lakes, pools, thermal springs and the ocean itself are regarded as places of pilgrimage and prayer where God and the holiest of spirits are most vividly present. The men and women who serve the water spirits carried considerable power, especially in Bantu Africa where the way of the water spirits is intimately involved with sacred kingship and queenship.

To clarify now before I move further, Bantu is not an ethnicity but a language group. Originating in the Nok region of Nigeria probably 2,500 years ago, the Bantu were never what is dismissively called a "primitive" culture. Likely by way of Nubia and the Sahel Corridor, presumably ultimately from Egypt, they spread the working of iron and the beauty and complexity of their world view over rather a large section of Central, South and East Africa from Cameroon to Kenya, from the Cape of Good Hope to Uganda. There are many Bantu languages and many Bantu cultures, and at the same time, they make a fairly coherent whole. They are certainly united around the sacredness of water, and I know of no Bantu culture where water does not play a central role.

Because of his fieldwork in West Africa and among the Dahomean diaspora in Haiti, Herskovits inevitably draws upon his understanding of the way of the water spirits from the sources he lived with. More recent scholarship has shown the overwhelming Bantu shape of African-American culture. It is when one looks at the water spirit tradition through a Bantu lens that the African shape of the black American soul comes into focus.

Before I get to the gist of the matter, let me explain why Bantu culture influenced the culture of the American diaspora to the degree that it has.

I'll begin first with the numbers, the percentages, that mind-numbing and terrifying way that we have come to measure human anguish. Philip D. Curtin estimates that by the end of the trans-Atlantic slave trade, roughly a third of African people lived outside of Africa, making the trade the largest forced migration in human history. About 4.5 percent of these ended up in the American colonies, the United States — roughly 430,000 people.

A rough estimate is that 40 percent of those sold in the slave ports such as Charleston, South Carolina, Savannah, Georgia and New Orleans were of Bantu origin. After the trade was made illegal in 1807, the "Kongo-Angola region became more and more important because the many channels and small islands at the Kongo River's broad mouth made it easier for the slavers to skulk out of sight of patrolling English and American warships." writes Richard Palmer. Well into the twentieth century, African-born Bantu speaking ex-slaves still lived in America.

Winifred Vass writes,

> For every slave landed alive, others died in intertribal warfare, deliberately instigated for the purpose of raiding, or along the trade route paths worn a meter deep into the earth that I have seen in Zaire. For every slave landed alive, others perished inside the stockades awaiting shipment or in the hold of the ships that made the perilous middle passage across the Atlantic.

After 1700, Georgia, the Carolinas, Tennessee and Mississippi maintained a black majority for over two centuries. Over two hundred Bantu place names in the South give a feel for the extent of the diaspora: Suwanee, Georgia; Loango, Alabama; Tuscawilla, Florida; Kolula Springs, Mississippi; Angola, Louisiana; Zacala, Virginia.

Aside from their numbers, "Bantu speaking slaves from Central Africa," writes Vass, "enjoyed a linguistic unity and ability to communicate with their fellow captives that slaves of West Africa did not share." Michael A. Gomez concurs:

> Once removed from the West Central African context and relocated to America, however, the Bantu languages and cultures, their treatment as a single people by their captors, and the need to effect strategies of resistance necessarily encouraged the Kongolese-Angolans to see themselves anew and forge ties of community.

These ties of community were further reinforced by the eth-
nic stereotypes that slaveholders carried about different African
peoples. Certain West Africans such as the Mande were thought
to make excellent "house negroes." Bantu, it seems, were best fit
for working the rice and indigo fields, the short-staple corn and
the cotton.

Given their numbers, the commonalities of culture and language and the work that ensured minimal contact with whites, it
should not be surprising that the nucleus of black American culture is strongly Bantu. However, there is a final reason, somewhat
more complex and rather difficult to state, that ensured a profound and subterranean continuity between Africa and America,
and it brings us once again to the mystery of the water spirits.

I will approach this from a rather odd angle, which is to say
from Zimbabwe.

Although Zimbabwe was not devastated by the trade like
the Bight of Benin or the coast and inland of Angola, nearly a
hundred shiploads of slaves departed from the Zambezi basin, and I have noted a few Shona words (Mandaza's tribe)
in the Creole language of Reunion in the Caribbean. Like other
Africans, Mandaza is given to speaking of the historical memory
of those bitter years:

> It is not only white people who were the oppressors. I also look
> at our own African chiefs who were in power during slavery.
> They allowed their own children to be bought. They said you can
> have this one or that one because you have given me a gown, a
> gun or a pair of shoes. These chiefs were cruel. They were also
> witches who collaborated with the white witches.

Like other parts of Bantu Africa, Zimbabwe was hugely influenced by Portuguese Catholicism and more currently Protestant
fundamentalism. A pattern that one finds throughout Central
Africa that had a profound effect on the shape of the African-
American soul is the persistent, intimate and paradoxical relationship between the way of the water spirits and Christianity.

There are at least as many Christians as traditionalists performing the rites of baptism at Victoria Falls in the sacred waters of the Zambezi. Both Christians and traditionalists share a Shona word for God, Dzivaguru, which translates as Big Pool, and Zulu Christians to the south refer to themselves as the "water church." Among our clan we dance to the Mambokadzi, the Queen of Water, but the song we sing is to Maria, the mother of God. The use of water for healing, the calling out for the falling of rain — one could pile detail upon detail. If it weren't for the fundamentalists' vulgar and dangerous assertion that the ancestors that traditionalists honor are actually demons, one might conclude that both religious domains are centered around the presence of God in water. Mandaza summarizes the traditionalists' point of view on the matter:

> Christ was a water spirit who took human form. That's why he was baptized by John. Secondly, he walked on the fish when he was possessed by water spirits. And remember, he also changed some water into wine. He said he was the living water.

This paradoxical intimacy between the way of the water spirits and Christianity was driven home to me during a conversation I had with Ambuya Magumbe.

Ambuya ("Grandmother") is a holy woman who, it is said, when she was young, lived in the village of the water spirits at the bottom of a river for seven years. Frail and now in her seventies, attended by her young husband, she carries the uncanny grace of a spirit medium who has given her whole self to God. Gathering a little snuff in the palm of her hand or extending a small gift to a stranger, her beauty is evident in even the slightest gesture.

Laughing at the girl she once was, she explained what it was like to come out of the river after so many years underwater. "The spirits were very heavy upon me," she said. "Very heavy," which is to say she felt quite out of her mind. Naturally she approached a group of Christians who might be able to alleviate the burden of so many spirits.

When they took her to a river to baptize her, she was trance possessed by a very powerful water spirit, and the Christians were so frightened that they took off running. She went to another Christian group. Again they tried to baptize, but the moment she went in the river, she was again taken by the spirits, and they too took off running. Exasperated, she tried a third group, but this time when the spirit descended, the Christians didn't want to offend such a powerful ancestor. They explained to Ambuya that it is not hers to follow the Christian path, that she must hold fast to the way of the ancestors.

And so she submitted to the endless work of being a vehicle for the spirits to communicate with their children but confessed to me that she hoped to return soon to the village of the water spirits.

What, one might ask, does this have to do with African-American culture? What could be more remote, more exotic to black Americans than this strange story?

Nowhere were the traditions of the water spirits and Christianity more profoundly intermeshed than in those parts of Central Africa — the Kongo, Angola and adjacent areas - that supplied the greatest number of Bantu chattel for the plantations of the South.

When the Portuguese first arrived in the kingdom of the Kongo, they were the objects of a serious case of mistaken identity by their African hosts. If the consequences were not so bitter, one could even imagine humor in it. Firstly, throughout Africa the ancestors are thought to be white, not white as in white people but white as in white spirits. The pale maggots that eat of the corpse, the whitening of the bones in the grave, the radiant light of God, the fact that black infants emerging from the realm of the ancestors during childbirth are exceptionally light skinned — there is no doubt that these things suggested the whiteness of the other world long before Europeans made contact, which is to say long before whiteness was racialized into a system of oppression. Mpemba is the Bantu word for the white kaolin clay found at the bottom of rivers that is used in the initiation rituals of the water spirit priests. It is also the name of the realm of the ancestors, and for contemporary Kongolese Christians, mpemba is heaven. Malcolm Guthrie's studies of the spread of Bantu languages indicate that as a word and a concept, mpemba has named the realm of the ancestors for at least two thousand years, which is to say that Bantu ancestral spirits have always been thought of as white.

Even before the Europeans arrived, the cross was the most sacred of Bantu symbols. It represented the meeting place of the world of God above, the ancestors below and the human village between.

For a coastal people who were not seafarers, it was believed that the white ancestral spirits lived on the bottom or on the other side of the Atlantic across the kalunga line that divides the worlds. So when Franciscan missionaries arrived on boats bearing an image of a water spirit nailed to a cross, practicing what was obviously an ancient version of the traditional rites of baptism, and preaching a gospel that reflected the way of the water spirits at its very best and, not incidentally, offering the possibility of mediating economic trade with their companions on the other side of the ocean, one can well imagine the intrigue in the court of the King of the Kongo.

It is not an exaggeration to say that what became African-American culture was born out of a dream or, more accurately, out of two dreams received the same night by two Bantu noblemen.

A year before Columbus sailed to the New World, shortly "after the first official Catholic priests arrived in Kongo," writes John Thornton, "two Kongo nobles dreamed simultaneously of a beautiful woman who beseeched the Kongo to follow Christianity. Moreover, one of them also found a stone which was 'black and unlike any others in the country' near his house which was shaped like a cross. When King Nzinga, a Nkuwu, heard these tales, he asked the Christian clergy present for an explanation. They unhesitatingly explained that the woman in the dream was the Virgin Mary and that she and the stone were 'signs of grace and salvation' and that the events were 'miracles and revelations.'" Nzinga a Nkuwu and his court soon accepted baptism and established a diplomatic alliance with his "royal brother," the King of Portugal as well as with the Vatican.

A century and a half later, Thornton continues, Queen Njinga of Angola came to the same crossroads. When she "was considering allowing priests to come to her base in Matamba in 1654-55 and convert her people, she sought the advice of the three spirit mediums (xingula) who served her. Each of the mediums was possessed with a different one of her ancestors, and she put the question of whether she should follow Christianity to each of the ancestors who spoke through the mediums. In each case the ancestor urged her to accept Christianity even though it meant that she would no longer follow the cult of the ancestors."

The story of the spread of Christianity across the Kongo and Angola is quite fascinating but also quite beyond the scope of this book. Nonetheless, few details need to be mentioned.

Perhaps to Queen Njinga's surprise, the Christianity that emerged in Central Africa simultaneously managed to preserve and encode the way of the ancestors even as it undermined and transformed it. In no way did Christianity defeat the way of the spirits. Quite the opposite: the spirits were incorporated into the ethos of Christianity, and an ancient way of knowing was preserved that might survive colonialism and the Middle Passage, that might even survive America. As a nganga, I have no doubt that this was the active intent of Spirit: Christianity was so completely saturated with the world view of the water spirit tradition that it became virtually an indigenous African religion. As Michael A. Gomez puts it, "It is the Africanization of the Christian faith, not its imposition by external forces, that accounts for its success in the African-American community."

"By the eighteenth century," writes Thornton, Christianity was the source of Kongo identity," and "virtually all the popu-

lation participated in and knew its rites and tenets." The rite
that compelled the new converts most of all was, of course,
baptism. Thus, he continues, "priests were regularly carried on
tours through villages of the country once a year to perform
sacraments (particularly baptism, which they performed by the
hundreds, occasionally the thousands)."

Thornton provides a terrifying and heartbreaking image of
this, that of the "bishop in Angola sitting on his throne in the
harbor of Luanda and baptizing hundreds of slaves by asper-
sion" before they embarked on the Middle Passage. The white
priests administered the sacrament, but the true vitality of Bantu
Christianity lay with the grassroots work "of maintaining an understanding of the faith . . . performed by large numbers of
catechists, who traveled more frequently, stayed longer and re-
mained at work even when there was no priest or missionary.
The fact that the catechists were African helped to ensure that
doctrine was 'naturalized' . . . "

This Africanization of Christianity was both encouraged and
punished by the Portuguese clergy. On one hand, the maxim
that governed the recent conversion of the European hinterland
("Whatever the heathens do is to be called Christian") was applied liberally as long as the "heathens" kept faith with the bare
bones of Catholic teaching. On the other hand, numerous diaries
and letters indicate that the clergy were perpetually frustrated
with the tenacity of African culture among "so-called" Christians.

Occasionally this frustration turned bloody as in the case of
the "Joan of Arc of the Kongo," Dona Beatrice Kimpa Vita. Led
by the spirits of two white children, she was eventually trance
possessed by Saint Anthony, and as the saint she would visit God
in heaven to bring his message to the people. "Although Saint
Anthony generally respected the missionaries and urged people
to support them and the Pope, the missionaries never had any
doubt that this was a diabolic possession," writes Thornton, and
so Beatrice/Saint Anthony was burned at the stake by the Office
of the Holy Inquisition in 1708.

To thicken the plot, the priests both deputized themselves and were widely accepted as ngangas. As Thornton writes, this "was fully equivalent to the Jesuits insisting on the behavior resembling that of Buddhist monks in Japan or Mandarin sages in China. They performed all the public and private roles expected of such practitioners in Kongo, from initiation ceremonies (baptism), to providing individual charms for luck (in the form of religious medals, thousands of which were distributed in Kongo), protection of fields by charms, performing public ceremonies to appeal to earth spirits in case of drought (with penitent processions, and self-flagellation) and consecrating the coronation of the king." (The rites of consecration had previously been the work of water spirit priests.)

It had also been the role of the water spirit priests to hunt out and destroy those "charms" (nkisi) that might be used in witchcraft. One would like to believe that these white ngangas, unversed in the subtleties of Bantu theology and no doubt regarding much of the native world view as witchcraft, did not comprehend the viciousness with which they were attacking the African soul by destroying nkisi. Nkisi, called in the American South "tobes," "hands," "mojo" were inspirited by the oldest of the ancestors, those upon which the coherence of the world relies. As someone of Catholic background, I would like to believe that they did not know what they were doing, but the evidence is that they did know because they named the Bible itself Mukanda nkisi and the church nzo a nkisi, the house of the ancestors. All of which is to say that these white ngangas, from a Bantu perspective, were acting exactly like the witches they were purporting to attack, and not surprisingly, a significant portion of the local people recognized them as such.

The bizarre and dangerous antics of a few deranged Franciscans didn't greatly distract the catechists from reinventing Christianity on African terms. It was they, not the priests, who ultimately determined the shape of black Christianity both in Africa and America. This is not to say that damage was not done.

I hear the echo of the damage every time I am told by a black American that Africa is uncivilized or that African religion is hoo-doo, a perspective that is all too common. Nonetheless, the water spirits have found shelter within the black church, "the sole surviving institution of the African fatherland" as W. E. B. DuBois called it. Eluding both Catholic manipulation and Protestant fundamentalism, these old spirits, wise beyond telling, recognized the spirit of Christ, knew it to be compatible with African wisdom and allied themselves with it to protect an endangered people from the unnameable cruelties of colonialism, slavery, racism — even from the church itself.

Just as the bishop of Angola blessed the slave ships as they left Luanda, so too did Father Pedro Claver dispense his blessings when the slaves arrived in the port of Cartagena, Columbia in the early seventeenth century. Most of the slaves believed they were victims of a form of systematic witchcraft and that they would be made into oil and eaten. The priestly robes could hardly be reassuring, having seen the behavior of the Catholic clergy in Africa. "Claver greeted every slave," writes Thornton, "embraced them and welcomed them to the New World, while constantly reassuring them that the Spanish intended to make Christians out of them and not oil." Father Alonso de Sandoval, also of Cartagena, was eager to save these wretched souls. He was surprised to find that almost all of the slaves from Central Africa were quite knowledgeable about Christianity and many of them were believers when they arrived.

One last historical "coincidence," the clincher, forever wed the water spirits to African-American culture.

The American colonies in the late eighteenth century were taken by a wildfire of evangelical activity known as the Great Awakening during which thousands of blacks and whites (often joined together in ecstatic praise) were converted by waves of Baptists, Presbyterians and Methodists. As it turns out, the Great Awakening coincided with the greatest influx of slaves from Bantu Africa, many of which had been well steeped in

Christianity and some of whom were, without question, cat-echists. Inevitably these became the avant-garde of black Protestantism. "Slaves were instructed," writes Thornton, "not by European clergy but by African Christians who knew their lan-guages and cosmologies intimately, and moreover had devel-oped formulae to convert one system to the other along the lines pioneered in Central Africa."

One of the more obscure words in American English is sim-bi, used only in the Georgia Sea Islands and the nearby coast-al areas. Simbi has the same meaning in English as it has in Haitian Creole, in Cuban Spanish, in Brazilian Portuguese, and in Kikongo. Simbi means "water spirit."

July Ann of Hatten, Mississippi sang the praises of God-in-Water when she was a slave in the early Nineteenth Century.

> "I was baptized in the Tangipaho River right here in Osyka, an' all de folks was shoutin' and I went down in de water shoutin' — I tell yo' I neber was so happy as I was dat day, an' I been a good Christian woman eber since I was baptized. I talks to de Lord an' his spirit tells me I am gwine to meet my Maker shoutin' — He tells us to shout for joy.

To be remembered by God. To be re-membered, literally put back together again by full immersion in water: Who exactly are the water spirits? As a nganga of the ngoma (drumming) of the water spirits, Mandaza understands why July Ann, even as a slave, found it in her to shout for joy.

> "These water spirits are the most powerful of all the spirits. They come out of the body of God, and they return to it. They are just like his angels. They say they communicate directly with God. They do not pray to any other spirits between them. They have got tremendous power of healing and wisdom direct from the Creator. They are water, they are air, they are clouds, they are rainmakers. This is what I understand about water spirits. These are the spirits that make use of me. It is these spirits who started telling me that they are healers, and they laid down steps I should follow in my healing.

30

2

CROSSING THE RIVER JORDAN

A couple of years ago I met Mansour Sow shortly after he arrived in America from Senegal. When I learned that Mansour was of Fulani ethnicity, I read to him from my copy of Holloway's AFRICANISMS IN AMERICAN CULTURE:

> . . . only recently have we begun to understand the extent to which cowboy culture had African roots. The annual north-south migratory pattern followed by the cowboy is unlike the cattle-keeping patterns in Europe but analogous to the migratory patterns of the Fulani cattle herders who live scattered from the Senegambia through Nigeria and Niger to the Sudan. Early descriptions of Senegambian patterns strikingly resemble later descriptions of cattle herding in the South Carolina hinterland.

Hearing this, Mansour smiled. "When I was a boy, I used to watch John Wayne movies at the cinema in Dakar. I'd watch the cowboys with their cattle, and I'd think how much like my people they are. Did you know that when the cowboys say 'Get along little dogies,' they are speaking Fulani? 'Dogies' is our word for calf."

I had a patient named Mr. Baldwin, a black man in his early seventies. We enjoyed engaging each other in wild and fascinating conversations about Africa and Lake Charles, Louisiana, where he came from. Once I read to him from Winifred Vass's THE BANTU SPEAKING HERITAGE OF THE UNITED STATES and found myself almost chanting a few of the nearly three hundred Bantu words that have made their way into American English:

ballyhoo, banjo, biddy, boohoo, boody, booger, boogaboo, boo-gie-woogie, bowdacious, bozo, conga, diddle, diddy-wa-diddy, flap-doodle, foofaraw, gee, goober, gumbo, hulla-baloo, hully-gully, jambalaya, jazz, jiggaboo, jive, kook, lallygag, loll, mojo, mooch, moola, mosey, paluka, poontang, ruckus, tote, yackety-yak, yam and zombie.

African culture clings closely to African-Americans, but they are not the only ones influenced by it. Robert Farris Thompson once said that if extraterrestrials were to scan the radio waves of planet earth and analyze the musical evidence, they'd like-ly come to the conclusion that the majority of human beings are black Americans. The Bantu trickster, Brer Rabbit, in typical trickster fashion it should be noted, found his way not only into American folklore and not only snagged in Disney's notoriously racist Song of the South but is incorporated into "a veritable saga cycle among the Cherokee" as well as the Creek, Natchez, Hitchiti, Seminole, Potawatomi and Koasati tribes who harbored escaped slaves. In addition, a few tribes in Brazil that had in-timate connections with the Bantu diaspora have long enjoyed hearing the stories of this notorious mischief maker.

My friend the African-American healer Tsehai Farrell speaks to why it is that few black Americans know about these things.

> The whole Bantu piece means recognizing the presence of the ancestors, that we are a part of something. Slavery made us think we were part of nothing. The African-American story as it is taught in schools is that we all began in a cotton patch. In my Transformation of Race groups, I find that's been people's first memory of who we are - the whole view cut short like we were nothing but head-rag cotton people, as if we started as slaves, no Africa mentioned.

I find the study of Africanisms endlessly fascinating, but al-though they are pervasive in the dream life of African-Americans, they are not the subject of this book. I am far more compelled by the mysteries that these "watermarks" point to, the survival of a culture and its particular way of understanding spirit and soul, an ancient way of understanding the universe and the soul's place within it. In this chapter I want to sketch something of the world view that African-Americans share with their brothers and sisters in the Motherland. This is merely a sketch: in working with the dream material, Mandaza and I will bring the fine details into focus.

Judith Gleason writes, "All things were created double, they say in Africa. Visible/invisible, male/female, the life-enhancing and the destructive — all phenomena partake of such dichotomies." I have found that this theme of doubleness pervades black American culture to a degree that is often not noticed at all or at least not worth commenting on so much is it a part of common sense.

Whenever I bring up the subject of dreams with African-Americans, more often than not I am told about futures foretold, messages from the Holy Spirit, visitations by angels or Grandmother or some dear friend that has passed, which is to say that my inquiries are answered in exactly the same way in the U.S. as they are by my friends in Zimbabwe. It is taken for granted that there is another side, a parallel and invisible world from which Spirit speaks; a world that offers structure, meaning, advice and wisdom; a world that one must have some relationship with if one is to make any sense at all of this life.

This other world is not the dream world, but dreams are an important way it reveals itself to us. Mandaza, for example, is dependent on his dreams and those of his patients to do the work of healing and initiating. Furthermore, as an herbalist, the spirits frequently come to him in his dreams to show him new plant medicines and how to use them.

> The spirits that formed you in your mother's womb come forth to meet the spirit of the herb. That is why spirit says everything that lives is holy. There is a community of spirits that is invisible, but in dreams they show their faces. Some are inside your body, and some are outside your body.

One time in 1996, for example, a dream told me to go to Victoria Falls and that my spirits would show me some herbs there. How that was going to happen, I did not know, but this dream said, "I am going to bring the herbs to you physically."

When I got to the falls, I saw a very big water bird carrying herbs in her beak and leaving them on a rock in the Zambezi. The river was low because of drought so I could wade out to the rock and collect the herbs. She came back with some more herbs, and I collected them also. Then she whistled and circled the place and disappeared.

That bird is called Mambokadzi. When I am trance possessed by her, I whistle just like she does. She is the Queen of the water spirits, and she is a healer. She knows all the herbs.

After I collected them, I returned to sleep, and she appeared again in the form of that bird and told me how to prepare those herbs. Here you see the relationship between the spirits and living things and the Creator himself.

Michaela Johnson is probably the only African I've met whose ancestors are African-Americans. Before being repatriated to Liberia in the last century, her great grandmother was a slave in Louisiana.

Michaela is a nurse's aide in the hospital I work in. Outside the room of a patient we were taking care of together, she told me about when she was visited by an angel.

Her mother in Liberia was very sick and had been so for weeks, apparently dying. Out of her mind with concern, Michaela decided to "do as the Bible says — fast and pray."

After several days of this, she returned home from a private duty case, graveyard shift, a long night of prayer. She ran a hot bath, climbed in, and quickly fell asleep. No sooner was she asleep than an angel, "whiter than white," silently wiped tears from her eyes. She woke up excitedly. Her sister was on the phone from Africa.

"Mama's all right, isn't she?" Michaela said.

"How did you know?"

Apparently Michaela's mother had risen from her coma during the night.

Art Patterson is a good friend, a fervent Pentecostal and a kind soul. Art had lost his brother, cut down in a drive-by shooting by a Mexican-American gang merely for being black. He told me stories of uncanny visitations, radiant and tender, when his brother came to him in his dreams. "I don't think I could have made it if my brother hadn't come back to visit a few times."

"Visitations" is the key word. To Western psychology it's obvious that water spirits do not exist. Birds are merely birds and do not talk, but should they talk in a dream, that may well be an interesting psychological fantasy worth exploring. Angels, of course, do not exist either, least of all angels carrying messages from the other side of the ocean. Neither do the dead return to comfort or instruct the living. Should you dream of the dead, a psychologist might encourage you to look into the inner meaning that the deceased carries for you: How does your brother represent an aspect of yourself?

I, for one, do not look forward to the day when workshops are set up to help people get in touch with their inner brother, their inner angel, their inner grandmother or their inner water bird. Western psychology has thoroughly dis-inspirited the world by placing everything of substance and meaning inside the self and thus neutralizing efforts to see exactly what the self is inside. Africans on both sides of the Atlantic tend to look at things differently: we live within a community of spirits, and without them we are lost.

Among the Bakongo one's dream soul is called mwela, which literally means "breath." It is paired with nsala, the seat of reason, the source of thoughts and ideas. Anita Jacobson-Widding explains, " . . . nsala and mwela together (being two aspects of the same soul) go to the land of the dead," both after actual death and after the ritual death of initiation. Mwela may "wander about when a person is sleeping," she writes. "When this person is dreaming, it is mwela that visits other places and tells the nsala of which it sees."

It is not only water spirits, angels and the dead that appear to the dream soul in times of crisis. So do the spirits of the living.

Carla Williams (not her real name) is a black Angeleno in her late thirties, a working class woman from South Central. Although a born again Christian, she often relies on my skills as a nganga, mostly dream work and the telling of cards.

Once when I was out of town, she came to a desperate crossroads. Bottoming out on cocaine, she hadn't slept for five days and was consumed with shame over the mother she had become and her irresistible desire for self-destruction. When she finally nodded out, she found herself at the end of a dark tunnel. My spirit appeared at the other end, urgently calling her toward the light. "Come on, Carla. Come on . . . " I said.

When she told me this story, I had her draw a couple of cards. What was my spirit drawing her away from? The Hanged Man, suspended between death and life. That was clear. And what was my spirit drawing her towards? Ten of Cups — the sacred marriage. With that we got practical. Three guys were sweet on her — which one? The cards indicated a coworker of hers was her soul mate. Not one to waste any time, Carla spirited out of town with this man that very week, and a couple of weeks later got engaged to be married.

In Zimbabwe it is Mandaza's and my nightly labor to defend the dream souls of our community. This we do as warriors. Occasionally in America I'm called to do the same, and this always makes me feel right at home.

Dreams are not the only way people receive messages from the sacred domain that is parallel to the world of the living. Intuitions, hunches and wild ideas are also honored with the proviso that one tries to discern the nature of the spirit speaking as one can easily be led astray. This is likewise true of "reading the signs," that mysterious poetry through which Spirit communicates through the medium of the natural world.

In Toni Morrison's novel BELOVED, Sethe and her teenage daughter Denver take off with Sethe's new lover Paul D. to check out the circus that's moving through town. It's Cincinnati, 1873, and Sethe and Paul D. knew each other as slaves but had been long separated. Denver was none too enthused by this new man friend of her mother's. On the way to the circus, Sethe notes that though the air is thick with tension and though she, Paul D. and Denver "were not holding hands, their shadows were." She took this to be a good sign. It was colored day at the circus, and Denver was ultimately buoyed up by Paul D.'s enthusiasm for the sight of "white people loose: doing magic, clowning, without heads or with two heads, twenty feet tall or two feet tall, weighing a ton, completely tattooed, eating glass, swallowing fire, spitting ribbons, twisted into knots, forming pyramids, playing with snakes and beating each other up." A good time was had by all, and "on the way home, although leading them now, the shadow of three people still held hands."

In traditional communities in Africa, one is always alert to small shifts and changes in any environment or in one's feeling life because Spirit is always looking for an opportunity to communicate with us. I remember sitting with Mandaza in the northern rain forests of Zimbabwe, and a lizard joined us, evidently quite attentive to our conversation. "Ah, there's one of my grandfathers," he laughed. Mandaza is ritually involved in rainmaking activity, and he routinely relies on signs like twitches in different parts of his body to gauge how successful he is in his efforts to talk to the clouds. More often than not, these twitches predict a rain shower long before anyone else in the community could see it coming.

One of the results of initiation is that one is awakened to the constant presence of signs and portents, and one sets out to refine one's skills at reading their meaning. But some people are born with "four eyes" (a term used both in Africa and the American South). I recall Mrs. Prichett, over eighty years old and the spitting image of Ambuya Magumbe. "I was born with a caul on my head in South Carolina," she told me, the caul itself being a sign of a child born with the gift of reading the signs.

Mrs. Prichett's psychic capacities were well received in her day, but that is not always the case. Black Americans carry a deep ambivalence for those with four eyes. Some regard it as a gift of the Holy Spirit; after all, the Book of Acts says, "your sons and your daughters shall prophesy, and your young men shall see visions, and your old men shall dream dreams." Others see it as the work of the Devil, altogether too close to hoodoo to want to have anything to do with it.

This was illustrated to me by Zora Walker and her twin sister Teresa. These two were afflicted by that quintessentially African disease, sickle cell anemia, and though I've never actually been with the two of them at the same time, their intermittent hospitalizations made it possible for me to befriend them each over the course of several years.

Zora and Teresa's mother was born with a caul on her head. Zora described her as a fallen woman (Teresa thought otherwise), and the two sisters were raised by their Jehovah's Witness grandmother in Oklahoma City.

Zora was greatly troubled by her own four eyes, her prognostitory dreams and her ability to see dark omens. In her grandmother's mind, it made her just like her mother, strange and somewhat dangerous. But while she was ashamed and tormented by her gift, she believed she was the good girl in the family and was quite committed to volunteer work with young people with the sickle cell trait. Her sister, Teresa, after all, was an addict and given to sleeping with a lot of men.

Needless to say, Teresa's point of view was somewhat different. Teresa never mentioned to me her sister's second sight, but she knew that she, Teresa, was grandma's favorite and had always stuck by the old woman and also by the mother, who had abandoned them as children. Teresa saw Zora as a hypocrite and goody-two-shoes. When the mother died, Teresa took to free basing cocaine in a serious way. "My sister didn't even mourn," she told me.

If anything, Teresa's dream life, though not quite as dark, was even more vivid than Zora's. In fact, I've never seen such wacky dreams in all the years I've been a collector.

This posed a few intriguing questions to me. Was it because of the sickle cell trait that these two had such amazing and lively intercourse with the spirits? Was it because of the massive dose of narcotics sicklers routinely use when they are in one of their crises? My informal inquiries into the dream lives of sicklers showed that, by and large, Zora and Teresa were exceptional. It was not until I was initiated into the spirits of sacred twinship that I was able to untangle the crazy threadwork of this family's story.

In Africa it is often the case that the gift of second sight and profound dreaming moves through the family line. Grandma's attitude sounds suspicious to me. Were there skeletons in her Jehovah's Witness closet? Had she herself seen things as a younger woman that frightened her? Had her kin? What did she think when she saw her daughter with a caul on her head? Of course, we'll never know the answer to these questions, but it is definitely relevant to take note that in Bantu culture twins (like albinos, epileptics and those with Downs Syndrome) are regarded as children of the water spirits because they embody the basic understanding of a doubled universe: They are born with a foot in both worlds. Mandaza's comment on an albino we passed on the streets of Mashvingo can apply equally to twins. "Those ones suffer so much, and they are very lonely. They will never be able to bear the spirits that call upon them if they are not initiated."

Before I can approach the question of initiation, it's best to explicitly state the original Bantu myth that laid the foundation upon which black Christianity relies for its understanding of the universe. Although there are many versions over Central Africa, they all share the primary image of what Wyatt MacGaffey calls a "reciprocating universe" — divided and mutually involved from both sides, from which Spirit reaches out towards humans to bring them into wholeness just as humans yearn to be completed by Spirit: the call and response of song, dance, dialogue and awareness. I paraphrase the old story as told by the Bantu anthropologist and nganga Fu Kiau Bunseki.

The Bakongo story is much like that of the ancient Greek myth of Hermaphrodites. The original being was both male and female. Its name was Mahungu and encircled the holy palm tree of god. Mahungu found itself divided in two, male and female, and created marriage as a way to recreate their original wholeness. This is the deep and underlying theme in traditional Kongo religion, making whole through the reconciliation of opposites.

It is said that the children of Mahungu suffered a terrible flood and famine, lost the sword of chiefship which kept intact the primordial order. What is left of the flood is the river Nzadi, often understood to be the Zaire River. The ritual and political heart of the traditional Kongo way is involved in calling into harmony that which has been divided by Nzadzi.

Dreams and the signs are Spirit's way of drawing us toward that reconciliation, that yielding to Spirit that African people call initiation.

Bantu and African-American Christianity preserved the central image of this old story: The river that divides the worlds is the most consistent and pervasive image in African Christianity both in the Motherland and the diaspora, but it is called by its Biblical name, the River Jordan.

In her study of the imagery of spirituals sung by American slaves, Olli Alho makes it clear that this mythical African river and Jordan are the selfsame body of water:

> The story in Exodus about the crossing of the River Jordan to the land of Canaan provided the composers of the spirituals with some of the most familiar allusions to getting to heaven. [Jordan, Jordan River, river banks (of the river), crossing over, sailing over, ship (of Zion)]. Just as mountain or hill may combine several biblical mountains into one mythical mountain, so the allusion river or crossing the river, may include, in addition, to the Jordan River, at least features of the Dead [sic] Sea.

In the spiritual "My Army Cross Over," from Higginson's collec-
tion, these two are combined with the "mighty Myo," the West-
African river of death:

> "We'll cross de might river
> My army cross over;
> We'll cross de River Jordan,
> My army cross over;
> We'll cross de danger water
> My army cross over;
> We'll cross de mighty Myo,
> My army cross over.
> O, Pharaoh's army drowned!
> My army cross over."

This extraordinary song, like so many others, manages to encode an African world that is coherent and outright militant. This
is African-American liberation theology at its best — spiritual liberation and liberation from slavery being one and the same thing.
It is not irrelevant that the slaves crossed the Ohio river to freedom and Harriet Tubman, called Moses, was said to walk on its
waters. Nor is it irrelevant that crossing the river that divides the
worlds is a primary way that Bantu people understand initiation.
One of the great gifts that black Americans have given the African
world is that they have transformed traditional Bantu theology
into a theology of liberation and have done so not only without
diminishing the tradition of initiation but actually opening it into
an expansive vision of human freedom from tyranny.

I do believe the above statements are true. In fact, I know
they are, but they are also lies because black Christianity has also
had the opposite effect of dividing blacks from African wisdom.
In the Motherland the attacks by Christians (and sometimes
Muslims) on traditional rites of initiation and the whole fab-
ric of traditional spirituality have been merciless. Large parts of
Africa are losing this essential knowledge passed from the elders
for thousands of years, and in other parts of Africa, these ways of
knowing are being thinned out, fragmented, made arbitrary in

ways that neither sustain nor engage the people. The Shona, for example, no longer initiate their young boys, and the Ndebele in Zimbabwe lost the tradition of bringing the young girls to womanhood a couple of generations ago. In America formal rites of initiation are almost unheard of among blacks. They are even becoming rare among Native Americans. This great melting pot of conformism, wealth, poverty and consumer aspiration threatens or commodifies ancestral wisdom traditions of every color and creed so that we have a country in which the very idea of "elder" is quickly becoming obsolete.

All this being said, the black and the white of it so to speak, I will contradict myself yet again by speaking "greyly." Rites of initiation do exist among American blacks. I hear the stories of them all the time. The deep story is archetypal and thoroughly Bantu. Whether it takes place in "the school of hard knocks" in an anarchic American fashion or is lived out within Christian, Muslim or other traditions, the soul, knowing its own spiritual slavery, will find its way to the banks of the Jordan River by whatever means necessary.

In Nigeria they say the trickster meets the soul at the gates of initiation — the master of truth telling and lying who informs the initiate that everything he or she knows is wrong. I do not mean to imitate the trickster with all my contradictions. I am not a good enough liar. It's just that the truth is so damn difficult to state without paradox. Spreading across time and space from the kingdom of the Kongo in the Fifteenth Century to the present moment, Christianity has both annihilated and preserved African tradition. Both. Simultaneously.

The soul, knowing its own spiritual slavery, will find its way to cross the Jordan River by whatever means necessary. Take Tsehai Farrell's story, for example — on one hand not typical of much of anybody (Tsehai is always, inimitably, Tsehai) but on the other hand bearing the basic structure of so many other stories I've heard from African and African-Americans.

Tsehai's rite of initiation into womanhood came when she was twenty years old. She was made Miss Watts when the black community was alive with nationalism in 1971. Naturally, the times being what they were, she was sent to Africa where she ended up in the court of Emperor Haile Selassie. Entering the spirit world and coming before the presence of the sacred king and queen is a common theme in many African rites of passage. Ethiopia was clearly the Promised Land, and it was where Tsehai first saw a specifically African world of grace and beauty. Before Selassie was deposed, Tsehai was engaged to marry into the royal family, but soon the royal family was overthrown, and her fiance was imprisoned. Tsehai's link with the Promised Land was cut off.

Twenty years later she replayed the story both to complete what was unfinished in that initiation and to submit to initiation as an elder and healer. Again the Promised Land beckoned. The spiritual head of a black Hebrew community saw what a remarkable woman Tsehai is and asked for her hand in marriage. She studied Hebrew, converted to Judaism, immigrated to Israel and lived in their community in the Negev Desert. The marriage was not one made in heaven, however, and after two years she returned to America.

For a black person to find the Promised Land in a racist country is never a simple matter. It was only when Tsehai was forty-two years old that she truly reconciled to the world she had always yearned for.

Crossing Jordan is always tumultuous, always a time of asking the impossible and necessary questions, a time of "identity crisis" and for Tsehai a time of great confusion and pain in relationship to her family. "What is my purpose in life?" she prayed. "Who am I? Why was I born to a family to which I have no deep attachments?" After a season of turmoil, she had a vision:

> I was observing a group of beings standing in holy council, gathered in a circle around something I could not see. They were explaining to an adult man, an initiate, a member of the council,

about what it was to be born and about his specific purpose in the life he was going to live. "You have a purpose," they said, "but when you get born, you'll forget it. You will forget, but there are ways to wake you up to the knowledge. Its not up to you alone to remember. Knowledge will come forth. We will synchronize events which draw forth your remembering at the proper time. This will happen in stages, but at some point, there will be a full blossoming, and you will remember us and what we said about your purpose. Until then we will remember you and lead you out of forgetfulness."

The vision shifted, and Tsehai realized that she herself was the initiate and that she was about to be born. The council offered their departing words. One, her lover, assured her that he would always be with her.

"I can't possibly forget you," she told the council. "I looked quickly at everybody and took a deep breath to take them into my heart and my memory and then stepped through the portal between that world and the world I was being sent to enter. On the other side of the portal, there was a long slide, and the vision ended with the good-byes becoming fainter and fainter as I slid into forgetfulness. It took me forty-two years to remember the scene."

Mandaza tells the story of his initiation in TWIN OF ANOTHER TRIBE, but a few details of it are so strikingly similar to Tsehai's story that they are worth mentioning here.

Mandaza was born into apartheid Rhodesia and, like Tsehai, he came of age during a time of great political turmoil over the matters of race. Politically involved as a young man in the fight against white supremacy, he was also a passionately religious Christian. He had been educated in a number of religious schools. As a poor boy wanting an education, his childhood was practically one of being a vagabond, wandering from one missionary school to another. Thusly he had acquired a gut level fear and antagonism to traditional Shona religion: "I didn't like it at all. I just didn't like it. I thought they were witches." Having been shaped by colonial Christianity at a young age (Rhodesian Christianity was very explicitly a tool of apartheid) made Mandaza's ordeal of crossing the river an exceptionally bitter one.

He was in his early forties (this being speculation since he doesn't know the year he was born) when the spirits came to call him home. For years he resisted this with everything that was in him.

This calling, this resistance is what Bantu people call sacred illness, in Mandaza's case, water spirit disease. The spirits choose an individual so that person can serve as a doorway for them to come into the world, to heal, to serve the community. Water spirit illness has particular symptoms that Bantu people recognize: an excruciating empathy for the suffering of others, mood swings, a sense of meaninglessness, stomach problems, feeling out of place wherever one is, money problems, vivid dreams and visions, irrational behavior, high blood pressure, being engulfed by guilt for the harm one has done, bad luck and a tendency to draw victimization to oneself. "The center does not hold." Tsehai's alienation from her family and the painful questioning about the meaning of her life are typical of people with water spirit illness. The only cure for this type of disease is initiation. Then the spirits sit in your body as allies and heal others through you.

At one point his boss, the headmaster of the school where he was teaching, said, "Young man, I must tell you there are very powerful ancestors working on you. You had better find somebody to initiate you."

"Aha!" Mandaza told me. "He started a war with that. I said he must never, never talk about ancestors working on me. No! No! But he insisted.

"'I don't believe in ancestors!' I said. 'They don't mean anything to me. I believe in the Creator who created the ancestors. This is my road. I believe in the Creator, the controller of the universe, not the spirits you are talking about. No!'"

Suffice it to say, things went from bad to worse. "I thought I was losing my mind." Physical illness, several car accidents, tormented by strange dreams, his wife leaving with the kids, be-

ing unable to stay awake at work, being reduced to utter poverty – meanwhile both friends and strangers, much to Mandaza's
great irritation telling him that his problems would not be re-
solved until he stopped resisting the call of the spirits.

Eventually he conceded, which opened up another chapter
of pain and futility. Several ngangas who tried to initiate him
failed. As he told me, reflecting back on it, "When my spirits
smell arrogance, they take off running." Then one night he had
a dream where he was approached by an Ndebele nganga, the
Ndebele being historical enemies of the Shona. Two days later
his work transferred him to Matabeleland, "enemy territory."

Three months after that, the nganga he had dreamt about
came to his workplace:

> He was just sitting outside on a bench. He approached me very
> nicely and said to me, "How are you?" We talked a lot. "Where did
> you come from?" – that sort of thing. Then he said, "You know,
> young man, you are not well."
>
> I said, "What do you mean?"
>
> He explained. "You have been having very powerful dreams,
> dreams which you do not understand. You have been to so many
> ngangas." Then he said, "Am I wrong?"
>
> I said, "Oh, no. You are right."
>
> The night before the initiation began, I saw in my dream a circle.
> This circle was in an African hut. Half of the circle was a group of
> old women. On the other side was a group of very, very old men.
> Some had long hair; others were bald headed, long bearded and
> so forth. But all of them were very old. I knocked, and they said,
> "Come in."
>
> Next to me was my uncle who had died recently, the one who
> had been struck by lightening. He said, "Come and sit next to me."
> I sat next to him, and he said, "You have come."
>
> I said, "Yes."
>
> And he said, "We are the ones who have been calling you."
>
> When I looked at them all, I fell down and started weeping.
> I wept for a long time, and when I woke up the following morn-
> ing, I was in tears.

In Africa, the realm of the ancestors — the world parallel to this one — is also the realm of the unborn. It is where our fate, our deepest sense of meaning, is determined before our birth. Initiation involves crossing the river to that timeless place to re-member our original purpose. We were born out of the world of the ancestors and return there in initiation to remember what we were born for. Thereafter we have a foot in both worlds so that when it's time to die, we know we are returning home.

Returning home is a theme that is very common in the old spirituals — "Swing low, sweet chariot, coming for to carry me home." Although most African-Americans don't believe in an ex-istence before birth like Tsehai and Mandaza do, I do find a pervasive sense that home is elsewhere, that this life, whatever its pain and beauty, is transitory and has no sustaining sense of meaning if its not lived in relation to a sacred world. The point here is not "pie in the sky when you die," but that the underlying meaning of this life emerges from relating to Spirit and in giv-ing oneself over to be a vehicle for the movement of Spirit in the world.

Mandaza and Tsehai's stories are uncommon ones, and yet every Sunday when it comes to "testifying," black Christians tell their versions of the same vivid tale of how they crossed over to Zion. "I was lost, but now I am found. I did terrible things, and I abused myself. My life had lost meaning, and I didn't know where to turn, and then God called me by my name. I resisted, and I resisted, and my problems got worse. Finally God won. I gave in, and you see before you a new person. I am not the person I used to be.

In the New Testament, the Greek word for this is "metanoia," translated as "conversion," but meaning literally "change of con-sciousness." In Africa, it's called initiation, and it is sustained by profound traditions protected by the elders to bring the soul to that crossroad where it yields to Spirit. If I had to translate into English, if I had to strip away all its African trappings, which in

America unfortunately "exoticize" it. I would say that the heart of initiation is the simple act of yielding.

There is a tough-minded and tender-hearted genius in African-American culture that can sometimes take the circumstances imposed by racism as an opportunity to transform poison into nectar. One finds an astonishing example of this in Candomble, an Afro-Catholic religion in Brazil. As in most rites of initiation in any culture, Candomble understands the necessity of ritual separation from the community which prepares the soul to meet Spirit. What I've called "crossing Jordan" is itself the organic process of breakdown and purification that by its nature isolates one from the community.

In Candomble the rites of separation so essential to initiation involved putting the initiate in the camarinha, a tiny windowless hut used to hold enslaved Africans. Here they were bound by ropes. In the camarinha the initiate undergoes the ritual death that leads ultimately to being reborn as a new person.

The soul that longs to be initiated, quite independently of what one would consciously choose, sooner or later finds itself confined in the camarinha. What I mean is this: Without the bitter and helpless recognition of one's own spiritual enslavement, one will never cry out to God or the ancestors, and one will never yield to the possibility of freedom.

Malcolm X found his camarinha in Norfolk Prison Colony in Massachusetts. He writes beautifully of this moment of yielding, death and rebirth:

> For evil to bend to its knees, admitting its guilt, to implore the forgiveness of God, is the hardest thing in the world. It's easy for me to see and to say that now. But then, when I was the personification of evil, I was going through it. Again, again, I would force myself back down into the praying-to-Allah posture. When finally I was able to make myself stay down, I didn't know what to say to Allah.
>
> For the next years I was the nearest thing to a hermit in Norfolk Prison Colony. I never have been more busy in my life. I still marvel at how swiftly my previous life's thinking pattern slid

away from me, like snow off a roof. It is as though someone else I knew of had lived by hustling and crime. I would be startled to catch myself thinking in a remote way of my earlier self as another person.

One way or another, in or out of prison, black Americans have had to find, develop and teach ways of transformation and spiritual freedom within the bowels of white supremacy. There is no River Jordan quite so deep and wide as the Atlantic Ocean. Respect demands that we consider the possibility that some in the hold of the ship and within the ordeal of slavery must have yielded to spirit for the sake of their children and their descendants.

There are four factors that make it virtually inevitable that at least some captives were able to take on the Middle Passage also as initiation.

First, for Bantu people of the coast and the inlying areas, the river that divided the world was not only thought of as Nzadi but also as kalunga. Kalunga is a word that has actually made it into the English of Barbados, meaning, according to Winifred Vass, "the sea, death, the grave, destruction, fate." In the Kongo, Kalunga also means God and the domain of the ancestors. Anyone who had been initiated before being enslaved knew that crossing the kalunga line meant crossing into the realm of the Spirit, that the ordeal of crossing over was excruciating but to live a life in relation to Spirit, the passage was necessary.

Secondly, the high percentage of water spirit priests meant that those who carried the deepest understanding of crossing over could be of assistance to those who were engulfed by the terror of it.

Thirdly, Michael A. Gomez points out that the slaving that served the American market "was distinguished by its relatively balanced sex ratios and high importation of children." It is an astonishing and unbearable fact that about one third of those enslaved were prepubescent children, which is to say children approaching that moment in their lives when their elders must initiate them. This is critical. It would be hard to overestimate its significance. Whatever the adults faced, everything in Bantu ethical sensibility insisted they maintain the role of elder for the sake of their children and ultimately for the sake of their descendants. A meaningless and dreadful ordeal had to be made meaningful, meaningful in an African fashion, which is to say, meaningful within the logic of initiation, if not on the ship, then within the institution of slavery itself.

Finally, and most importantly for African people, it is a given that when one cries out in anguish, Spirit comes forth on behalf of its children. This moment of crying out is the very essence of prayer. It is the turning point. It is when one learns the meaning of prayer. Whether it was a catechist crying, "Why hast Thou forsaken me?" or a priest of the water spirits calling out to the ancestors, without prayer the Middle Passage would have efficiently snuffed out the souls of those who were to be the first African-Americans.

I truly do not wish to romanticize this or craft a superficial fantasy of the heroic slave. At the bottom of initiation, a shattered self faces a shattered world, and the ancestors come forth not with answers but with questions: these ones, these children, these seeds of the future generations — how do we serve their spirits? What is asked of us now? Questions that the ancestors must have asked themselves, just as they insisted the captive Africans interrogate their own souls.

If one sees this as the ancestral lineage of African-Americans, it clarifies why black Americans, even on the level of their dreams, remain African. It also explains the curious fact of the pervasive influence of black American culture on contemporary African music, politics, religion and theology because some of the ancestors that come through African-Americans, far from being orphaned spirits, were profoundly initiated by historical circumstance. It also casts the camarinha ordeal and Malcolm's initiation in prison in a new light, for as the Yoruba say, "If we stand tall, it is because we stand on the shoulders of many ancestors."

3

PRAISE SONG FOR MAPATYA

I am moved to sing a praise song to my twin and the spirits we serve. Let me begin with a story.

It was Easter morning in Bulawayo. The previous night I had given Mandaza a gift, a small desert stone striated with the fossil of an ancient fern. Knowing how much Mandaza loved the story of Moses (he named his little boy Moses), I had purchased this stone from an old Bedouin man at the foot of Mt. Sinai.

Mandaza, being Mandaza, tends to use gifts as opportunities to heal, if that is at all possible. That morning he gathered his children, Simakuhle and myself in the house of the spirits. Mandaza had ground the stone to dust and mixed it with leopard fat and herbs. He had Simakuhle make tiny cuts in our wrists into which he smeared the medicine. This ritual had been part of my earlier initiations. The spirit of Sinai, the majestic solidity of the Law, was now in the bodies of myself and his family.

When we returned into the main house, the television was on, and Brenda Fawsie was belting out gospel music in English and Zulu – a bilingual song completely infused with the spirit of black American gospel. We all took to dancing, the whole family, and I soon found myself weeping freely - an extraordinary moment of seeing the genius of African-American people ecstatically received in the Motherland. Mandaza started singing along with Brenda. "Soon and very soon we are going to see the king, hallelujah, hallelujah, we are going to see the king." I've rarely seen him more beautiful. "What can I do but sing?" he said. "Some of my spirits are Christian."

It's true. Mandaza has Christian spirits. They sure do love Jesus, those ones, and are in every respect pure of heart and wanting only to serve the Lord. I have a special friendship with one of my mapatya's Jewish spirits, who likes to argue Torah. He is reflective, serious, a deep soul who finds the idea that Christ is the son of God a bit absurd, a theological blemish on the integrity of monotheism. This spirit will even quote the New Testament to make its point.

Like the Jewish spirits, Mandazas' Muslim spirit has food taboos. He has Mandaza buy his chicken at the Muslim butcher "because they pray over it," that is to say, when he's not getting it from Mrs. Goldblum who runs the kosher meat market, both traditions, as it happens, using the same prayerful slaughterers.

Then there are the kings: Chapungu, the black eagle, such a fierce warrior and so deft in the arts of peacemaking; the white eagle; the lion; the mermaids, who are so coquettish and giggle a lot and who insist Mandaza eat neither fish nor pork; the old nganga who is a hunchback and in constant pain; Mambokadzi herself, who speaks in whistles; the peacemaking spirit who has no name and is something of a vagabond saint; various grandfathers, at least one of them white ("Oh, yes, I have white spirits just as you have black spirits") and grandmothers and, oh, yes, Ambuya Buwebuwe, Grandmother Spider. She is wonderful, wise, exquisite in her movements, as old an ambuye as there could be. It is she that relates all these spirits to each other and connects them to the work of healing, which is the work that Mandaza seems to be involved in during all his waking hours and throughout his sleep as well.

Is Mandaza psychotic? Does he have a rather severe case of multiple personality disorder? Or merely an extremely hyperactive imagination? These are irrelevant questions, really, if you "think in Bantu." These spirits existed before Mandaza was born and will long outlive him. He has merely made his life hospitable to whatever spirits want to make use of him. "I am God's legs," he says. "God's hands. How else is God going to act in the world if I don't let him come through?"

Temperamentally Mandaza is one of the friendliest and most approachable people I've ever met. He interacts with beggars and pickpockets with much the same warmth as his friends in the police force. (Mandaza was in the police force for thirty years until he retired to become a full-time nganga.) Most every interaction, either by direct intervention or simple kind presence, he meets with the intent to heal. I remember sitting in a real estate office with Mandaza across from dear Mrs. Esnath, a matronly white realtor from one of Bulawayo's more prestigious families. We were doing business, but Spirit moved Mandaza to tell this women her dreams and advise her on her problems — problems, mind you, that Spirit seemed to know a lot about even though Mandaza and I had just met the woman and she had shared nothing private with us at all. She was remarkably receptive and didn't even betray perplexity that this African stranger understood her so well, knew even her dreams. All in a day's work, ordinary enough to Mandaza that he didn't even mention it as we left her office except to say, "I really like that woman. She is a fine human being."

What Mandaza carries is the African genius for multiplicity. He does not march to a different drummer, he dances to any number of drumbeats, and he does so with extraordinary style and panache. He takes the circumstances of civilization and turns them on their heads. His king and queen spirits serve the poor people of Bulawayo. They do not lord over them but regard serving the poor as the essence of nobility. His Christian spirits dance happily alongside Muslims, Bushmen, and white grandfather spirits without a trace of colonial bigotry.

Much of my various initiations have been about being taken into the family of Mandazas' spirits and vice versa, he being taken into mine; so I feel a fondness for these invisible ones that whisper in my ear; some of them trance possess me also when I don't know how to address the suffering I see in others. I try to remember who I was before initiation, but it's a bit hard to think in the same fashion as I did then. I realize, looking back, how simple I was though quite infatuated with what I took to be my complexity. When Mandaza said that some of his spirits were Christian, I thought about my endless self-involved pre-occupation with my biracial background, my Mexican Catholic mother, my white Anglo-Saxon Buddhist father and how I tried to make sense of this in an all-American binary language. This always opened up labyrinths which endlessly fascinated me even as they bored me (and my loved ones) to tears. Am I Catholic? Or ex-Catholic? Is it just the sacrament I love though I despise the Church? Am I really Buddhist and not Catholic, my father's son or my mother's? Am I a heretic Buddhist, a forest yogi or a Zen idiot? Or have I Africanized Tibetan tantra?

All of this may sound very complicated, but really it was not. It was always a refusal of plurality. I had to be something — either/or or both. And whatever I was, I had to take it very, very seriously because that was my "identity," and if I couldn't define my "identity," pin it like a butterfly and appreciate its various qualities, then I really wasn't anybody. Again, either/or — I'm either somebody (definable) or nobody.

Mandazas' plurality is quite blissfully beyond this. He cares quite a lot about how to surrender to God and how to be useful to the world, but if his identity or lack of it concerns him, he's never mentioned it to me.

Mandazas' plurality is a profoundly African quality. A patient of mine, Mr. Mernit, once told me about when Ella Fitzgerald and Louis Armstrong were in Africa and visited the pygmies. "Ella and Louis," he said, "heard them sing in eight-part harmony. Eight-part harmony! Here we have three- or four-part harmony but eight?"

54

The Swiss polymath Jean Piaget came to the conclusion after years of studying the cognitive development of children that between the ages of four and seven, the very height of human intellectual capacity is achieved. "Reversibility thinking" is the ability to place three or more contrary possibilities alongside one another without insisting that merely one of them be true. Most people lose this capacity for imagining multiple possible truths by the time they are seven. My friend Judith Remington calls this para-epistemology, the ability to engage different and contradictory ways of knowing. Mandaza carries this even further. His spirituality is characterized by moving in and through and between any number of ways of being and seeing — all for the sake of healing. Mandazas' sense of logic can only be called polyrhythmic.

Apocalypse is a relentless assault on intelligence: the supple intelligence of children, the multiplex intelligence of indigenous people, the heartbreaking and interinvolved intelligence of whole ecosystems. In such a situation, the pathologies of power come to the fore, which cross-culturally means the pathologies of male power. African epic stories are filled, like European stories, with mad kings and reigns of tyranny. And like Europe, Africa has a tradition of bards (griots) and fools whose sacred task was to make fun of the king, perhaps, sometimes, get him to reflect on himself. When I read Mandazas' tarot, I'm surprised at how often he chooses the Fool. Yes, the Fool mocks the king when he has become a tyrant, but the Fool also is the one who steps off the cliff, perpetually giving himself over to the unknown. Mandaza in Botswana now being initiated by the Bushmen is such a Fool. And myself? As for me, I can only ask that those who have followed me and my mapatya this far take with us, please, the next step into the dreams and nightmares of African Americans.

God gave Noah the rainbow sign
No more water, the fire next time

Old Spiritual

Fire spirits are the warriors. For them red is not an
evil color. They bring fire to burn out the rubbish.
And when the rubbish is burnt, it turns into water.

Mandaza

LIKE A MOTHERLESS CHILD

4

REMEMORY

Mandaza says, "There is an apartheid in our waking lives, but in the spirit world there is also apartheid where white spirits come and oppress. On the spirit level slavery still exits. It exists so much more so than in the last century. There are so many people in America who have these dreams about slavery."

You get up in the morning late. The alarm clock doesn't go off, or perhaps you forgot to set it. You have to rush to work, a job you despise, but it's work. Breakfast, such as it is, is black coffee and toast with margarine Would you call this a "racist" breakfast? Do you notice the taste of blood in the coffee, perhaps the blood of Guatemalan Indians who have no land to grow corn to feed their children but work the plantations so they can enrich already wealthy Ladinos and who have been tortured and killed by the tens of thousands for protesting this arrangement? And the margarine? Not butter really, but who can afford butter?

Margarine was invented in the last century by an eccentric amateur chemist, but it wasn't until the 1920s that anybody could see any profit in manufacturing it. When it was discovered that one could make a killing in using palm oil as a cheap ingredient, factories were set up in Malaysia and West Africa.

West Africans used palm oil for their own purposes, both cooking and ritual activity. The trees belonged to the ancestors, and the oil was one of their gifts to the village. The men would pick the palm nuts, and the women would process the oil. But what is one to do when foreigners come, set up plantations and factories, bring in a cash economy, and the only way to survive, suddenly, is to work for the Europeans? The village begins unraveling. The old way of harvest had a kind of poetry to it within which one remembered the ancestors and felt grateful to them. No more. The balance in the dance of gender, maintained since before anyone could remember by the harvesting of palm nuts, has been thrown into chaos. Men get confused and therefore arrogant or depressed. Domestic violence increases.

Can you now taste the rage of these men and the terror of these women who they'd like to love but cannot remember how?

Leonard Cohen sings, "Everybody knows the deal is rotten, Old Black Joe is still picking cotton for your ribbons and bows. Everybody knows." Bantu medicine takes this further. Racism and the economies that thrive on it is a systematic form of what the Shona call muti. Soul-eating. Witchcraft. Hoodoo. It is pervasive and so much the stuff of everyday life that it is invisible, very often invisible to blacks as well as whites. Dreams often bring the invisible reality of this system before our eyes so we can engage in the work of freeing the Spirit.

When I first began reading Mandaza the nightmares of black Americans, the fury of the warrior would rise up, and he'd reach for bute, the sacred snuff, to cool himself down so he wouldn't be trance possessed during my interviews. As a healer, Mandaza is in many respects first and foremost a warrior — especially when he intimates the helplessness of a soul that is being eaten.

Since the sixties, discourse about racism in America, with some brave and notable exceptions, has become both superficial and hopelessly predictable. Among whites — I mean here white liberals — it's as if racism was about having or not having good or bad feelings about people of color. The realities of the inner city, distant and horrible, fill every decent soul with pity, but who takes time to reflect on the organic relationship between poverty and affluence? And having reflected, who acts?

"Pity would be no more." says Blake. "if we did not make somebody poor."

James Baldwin, compassionate and utterly no nonsense, wrote about how irritated he would get at the sentimentality of the civil rights movement. Among blacks nowadays, I see very little of that sentimentality when it comes to race though it is alive and well among some whites who'd be delighted to join hands and sing "We Shall Overcome" or "We Are The World." The invention of a viable black middle class now masquerades as the solution to racism. Yes. Necessary. Opportunity, of course. But does this even recognize or alter the system of soul-eating? The middle class of all races imagines a utopia outside of the bitterness of historical circumstance: looking for love in all the wrong places. But there are countless ways to serve one's soul up as a banquet to the witches just as there are countless ways to eat the soul of another. On the level of the dream, there is no evidence that the lives of middle class blacks are exempt from racism eating at the souls.

"I don't hate the white man, really. I hated the system, this evil system. I prayed in those days of apartheid that such a system would come to an end peacefully," says Mandaza. About the system Mandaza is uncompromising, and about it he does not lie. Born into its own particular hell, taught by missionaries to despise his ancestors, coming of age during a racial war — white against black and black against black. This was his introduction to the system of racial oppression: bloodshed; tending the wounded; tattooed on his forearm as a teenager so the police could monitor his movements during the war and then recruited against his will into the police force; his mother's leg and hip blown away by a land mine; his family cracking under the strain of poverty and war; and Mandaza being the vagrant son because he returned to tradition and, unlike many of his kin, no longer a Christian; pariah, treated as if he himself was possibly a witch. "I don't hate the white man really. But the system is evil." And the system, as far as Mandaza can tell from the dreams I read him, is substantially the same in America as in Zimbabwe. It is, indeed, global.

I invite the reader into the camarinha — as an initiate, I suppose, but firstly as a slave — bound, humiliated, broken and endangered at the level of soul.

In the Bantu spirit world, such a thing as slavery remains intact until all the slaves are free — all the spirit slaves. Neither the Emancipation Proclamation nor even death itself necessarily liberated the slaves. There is a world outside of time, parallel to our day-to-day lives, altered by initiation, prayer and insight but not necessarily altered by what we do "in time." The past, the present and indeed the future come together in the work of spiritual liberation.

For the Bantu, the ancestors are not exactly "dead": they are not of the past, or rather, they are also of the past but vividly here now as much as you and I are here. Our welfare — as individuals, as a community — depends on their welfare. So to say the ancestors are enslaved or their souls are being eaten is to say we ourselves are unfree. Our freedom depends on theirs. Initiation, among other things, is the freeing of the ancestors from the house of bondage.

In Bantu medicine it is the responsibility of the living to heal the ancestors, to liberate them. When our spirits are "down," when we feel unfree, it is because they are unfree, oppressed. We are made free and whole just as they are because they inspirit us. Mandaza makes this clear in his explanation to Bruce Abrahami, an Afro-Celtic musician we initiated together in Zimbabwe:

> Your ancestors wanted you to actually bring them back home. They saw your love, the patience and understanding in you who were innocent.
>
> And they said, "This is the man who can bring us back home. We can protect him. We can rebuild the home that was abandoned and destroyed."

You, in turn, tell them, "You can use me as your vessel. I am ready. Come back and rebuild the ancestral home for it has been broken and its bricks scattered."

They knew that in your heart they could find a new home and be at peace and forgive the evils done to them.

Bruce's ancestors were Jews who had inhabited Kurdistan since the time of the Babylonian exile. His great-grandfather, by way of divorce, threw his wife out of the house, and she and her sister joined a caravan to cross the desert and find a home in Palestine. On the Turkish frontier, they were waylaid by brigands, raped and murdered. Mandaza recognized immediately that Bruce's troubles in this life were not personal; they were ancestral.

This idea of a parallel world is expressed beautifully by Toni Morrison. Sethe tries to explain to her daughter, Denver, how it is that though emancipation has happened in history, in the spirit world the plantation is present and unchanged.

> Some things you forget. Other things you never do . . . Places, places are still there. If a house burns down, it's gone, but the place — the picture of it — stays, and not just in my rememory, but out there in the world. What I remember is a picture floating around out there outside my head. I mean, even if I don't think it, even if I die, the picture of what I did, or knew, or saw is still out there. Right in the place where it happened . . . Where I was before I came here, that place is real. It's never going away. Even if the whole farm — every tree and grass blade of it dies.

Denver asks if other people can see it, and Sethe replies,

> Oh, yes. O yes, yes, yes. Someday you be walking down the road and you hear something or see something going on. So clear. And you think it's you thinking it up. A thought picture. But no. It's when you bump into a rememory that belongs to somebody else.

Henry Cheatam, an ex-slave from Mississippi, confirms that for those who suffered being human property, the story was far from over even after emancipation. Slaves, he said, were "all superstitious and fear that the slave driver, having whipped so much when alive, will somehow be beating them when dead. I was actually as much afraid of my old master when dead, as I was when he was alive. I often dreamed of him, too, after he was dead, and thought he had actually come back again to torment me more." Slaves, he said, "preferred to be buried the greatest possible distance away from their master." Another slave, Louis Clark, "watched two of his fellow slaves dig their master's grave six or seven feet deep and then helped them place a large stone on his coffin so as to fasten him down as strong as possible." Measures such as this are common when burying witches in Central Africa.

The plantation is real. It is collective. It lives, invisible, within the circumstance of life in contemporary America.

Andrea Matthews and I corresponded for a couple of years. She had read an article I had written on race and dreams and sent me a couple of dreams of her own. Where she is now I don't know, but when she had this dream, she was getting her Ph.D. from a university in East Texas.

> I was living in Oklahoma, but it was like the Old West, and the town was run by Mormons. One side of town was full of blacks and Mexicans — that's where I lived — and we were the slaves of the white folk. We had things — radio, television and stuff — we weren't hungry or anything, but we also weren't free to leave. Some of us decided to escape. This was hard. It was like the whites had eyes everywhere and would watch our every move. We broke into a store to get supplies to take with us, but a big white dog came into the store slobbering, and two white men blocked the door so we were trapped.

This dream disturbed Mandaza greatly. Some dreams seem to speak only to the individual, but according to Mandaza, dreams about enslaved spirits speak to the world at large. The dream soul is able to perceive where we are at collectively.

This one here is a dream that comes from a very powerful spirit. It is the Creator's message to the people not only of that particular area. What did she call it? Oklahoma? But to the other areas where apartheid is still being practiced. There is oppression here of the weak. There is poverty manipulated by those who have the power and the means. This dog here is an evil spirit. These white spirits that are still keeping black slaves are what I would call in my understanding witches because they are enjoying the wealth they've got by means of suppressing others and making them suffer. This is definitely a warning dream from the Creator himself saying, "What is it you are doing among these people?" In this dream I see not only America but the world.

This happens in Zimbabwe, too. The witches will put a person's soul in a bottle and plug it up. And then they eat it at their leisure. They make a world that traps blacks. White eyes everywhere! Ah! Look at that store — no way out. And the witches give the blacks toys, televisions and what-what. They have created a situation where they think blacks will say, "This is a good life within oppression. You can have a good life as long as you give up your freedom."

It seems as if Andrea's dream soul perceived higher education as a world defined by whites, a place of entrapment, a place where the soul is endangered. Or perhaps her ancestor spirits found university somehow familiar — yes, of course, not exactly the plantation but similar enough to draw the dream soul into "rememory" of that world that remains intact until all the spirits are free. Malcolm X understood well the ambiguity of the "house negro," who by fortune or fate would work in the master's house instead of the fields; learn his particular language (in the university heavily Latinized, abstract and without soul); be given certain advantages through proximity to the white world; be envied by the "field negroes"; yet in no way given anything that could be called freedom. In America this is a particular niche within which the soul is eaten.

Andrea did not succumb. She learned two languages: the language that legitimized her as an intelligent human being in the eye of the master and the language of soul. I believe a trickster spirit came to her aid, teaching her the subtle art of switching languages, switching selves so her soul would not be eaten.

It was Nikki Tremont's dreams that led Mandaza to speculate that many American blacks carry water spirits. Like Andrea, like many water spirit people, Nikki dreams not only for herself but for the community at large. And like many people with water spirits, she is given to nightmares, both because her dream soul sees things too clearly and because water spirit people are prey to those spirits that seek to undo human goodness. Nikki had this dream in high school in Los Angeles not long after the city burned following the Rodney King verdict.

> I was at my high school where, you know, most of the students were white. I knew that the school was built on top of the bones of black people and that blacks were being killed and buried secretly beneath the buildings. I tried to tell this to people, but nobody believed me. They acted friendly and all and just wanted things to continue as if everything was normal.

Mandaza's comment is simple and to the point: "She is being shown that the whites need to look upon us as friends, but down below their hearts, they are massacring blacks. She is carrying a secret knowledge that witchcraft is happening."

Higher education or high school — in both situations the soul is endangered. The soul is encircled by the Great White Lie: Everything is normal. Why are you being so paranoid? In fact, when Nikki had this dream, she was confused at the refusal of the white students and teachers to talk about the uprising that had just occurred, as if it were an irrelevant event, as if they had happened in a far-off country and were as forgettable as yesterday's news. The need for normality, for business to proceed as usual, is a particularly devious kind of soul-eating.

Again, the dream soul enters the rememory of the plantation. How much the master needs his blacks to be happy and content, or failing that, to be quiet.

Teenagers with water spirits have it particularly hard because in the teenage years one's soul is between the village and the bush, on the edge between being domesticated and wild. This is the time for initiation for it is when, on every level of one's being, the ancestors are coming forth with their complex questions and their terrifying lucidity, bringing dreams such as Nikki's which nobody wants to hear. Nikki's dream soul knew that she was in a world without elders, without anyone to confirm her perceptions and help her shape them. She knew she could well end up buried beneath the school herself if she didn't learn to preserve the veneer of normality. That black teenagers are driven out of their minds or over the edge into violence by a culture that imagines itself to be normal is one of the truly tragic realities of our time. Having taken refuge in her gift for acting, Nikki, like Andrea, is surviving.

Tamika Carter is a secretary at the hospital where I work. In her early twenties, she had this dream when pregnant with her first child by her Mexican boyfriend.

> I was in a park pushing my little baby in a stroller, and these two white men came and tried to steal my baby. I cried out for my father to come and help.

Mandaza sees this dream as a rememory of slavery, an attempt to capture and enslave the spirit of the next generation.

> The powers that were there in this particular era created little worlds. They had worlds of white people which were rather private and a second world which is public where the oppressed could be exposed to any danger. When I look at this child being taken away from its mother, this is during the slavery period. People were snatched from their relatives, and the children were crying to their fathers, "Give us protection, we are now being taken away." This dream is another warning message to the world for as long as you still collect your little worlds amongst your people, how can you be able to talk to God? There is going to be chaos. The two white spirits that tried to capture this child are witches, very greedy. They wanted cheap labor; so they were

forcing people to work for them. The witches in this dream want to eat the blood of these children, eat their sweat, eat their energy, eat their freedom. They are stealing the soul of this child to take it away and eat it through labor. That child was going to spend all of his life sweating for his master. It is the child that brings the dreams to this woman, saying, "I want to be free and return to my village." The work of the nganga among African-Americans is about freeing these spirits so they can return home.

Mandaza's statement is complex. The shifting between past, present and future may look confusing, but the realm of the spirits is timeless though it affects time. This unborn child carries an ancestral spirit that is a slave. As we say in America, the child is an old soul. For the sake of the child, the ancestor must be liberated, protected, returned to a world that makes sense; otherwise, the child runs the risk of growing up believing that he or she is unfree at the root of his or her being.

In Zimbabwe there are rituals to send slave spirits home where they become protectors of the village, warrior spirits. In one of my initiations, a slave that my ancestors kept was removed from my body and sent home, and as a result, my soul was no longer snared in recycling the endless drama of master and slave. But America is not Africa, and there are other, quieter ways of returning the spirit home. Home is here. It is where the heart is, and the birth of a child is always incentive to enter into the labor of an adult – entering into the give and take of reciprocity, of making a family and around that family a village. Sustaining that village alongside others so these old souls can find a measure of freedom in an unfree world is essential to the art of parenting. In this context, it is worth saying, before the old proverb is made into a cliche, it does, indeed, require a whole village to raise a child. Without the village the child is prey to witches, is unprotected, is likely, again, to be enslaved.

Mr. Cary, whose dreams first showed me that black Americans were dreaming whites in the same way that Bantu people do, sent me this one:

> I dreamed that I was on a large stage screaming at the top of my voice, and there were all these white folks looking up at me, and their eyes merged into one eye that hovered above me.

Mandaza sees this dream, again, as a rememory of slavery:

> The village of this dreamer here was surrounded by white soldiers. The people of this village were captured, shouted for protection from their white invaders. The white witches are encircling this man, and he is all alone. The whites are focusing on this village — the eyes again! Eyes like this eat souls. "Let us capture this village," the whites say. "We have one mission together."
>
> This man I would take into deep initiation and clear away the obstacles. He needs some help here. He needs protection from his spirits. In this particular instance, his ancestors are helpless. They are not giving any protection at all.

Mandaza knows what it is to be surrounded by white soldiers, having witnessed a massacre at his school when he was a teenager. He also knows from his own experience what it means to move through this life raw and stripped of any kind of spiritual protection in a world that is manifestly dangerous. Mr. Cary and Tamika's dreams express a common theme in the dream life of African-Americans, a theme Mandaza explicitly traces to the rememory of slavery: being attacked and being spiritually defenseless to do anything about it. To this recurring theme of defenselessness, Mandaza returns repeatedly to the necessity of initiation. Initiation, among other things, gathers to the soul the spirits of protection.

Being unprotected is a theme I have found to be common among blacks of whatever social stratum, from homeless to well-to-do, but among black men in prison, it seems to be routine. Prison itself is clearly at the front lines of spiritual warfare. It is in prison that black Americans return most completely to the hold of the slave ship, to the camarinha, to the spiritual trial that either transforms them or devours their soul.

George Knowlton was a prisoner at Attica, upstate New York. Maintaining an old and honorable tradition, being one of the few surviving Marxist-Leninists in America, he gently suggested I interpret his dreams according to the principles of dialectical materialism. The three dreams that George sent me were all about being assaulted and unprotected. On one occasion, he leapt from a dream, shouting, "Stop this psychological warfare bullshit," and kicked the bars of his cell and broke his foot. But George's dreams of being unprotected far precede his ordeal of doing time. When he was eleven years old, he dreamt:

> I was at home with my little brother, and these two big white gangsters, Al Capone types, broke in the door. They tried to flush my little brother down the toilet. I tried to stop them, but I just woke up in a panic.

Mandaza's comments reflect how it is that some dreams belong to the family or perhaps the world.

> The spirit that protects the whole family is on this boy who is dreaming. He must be initiated so he can fully do the work of protection. If he does not get initiated, the family is endangered. He is their salvation. He knows what's happening on the spirit level, that his little brother is endangered. He couldn't help his little brother because he's not initiated.

Mandaza's response surprised me. "You would initiate a little boy?" I asked.

"Oh, yes. We would initiate him. If his brother was flushed down the toilet, he might die. That is the way it is with witches. Suddenly children die or other family members, like poisoned rats. They have no protection at all."

Mandaza's perspective here is reinforced by something I once heard Dr. Aminifu Harvey say when he was discussing his work of initiating black gang members in Washington, D.C. Being a light-skinned black and an academic, Dr. Harvey is in many respects a fish out of water when he goes to the inner city. Once he was on the streets there with his teenage daughter and came

upon a small group of homeboys that he recognized. He introduced his daughter and appealed to them not as violent young
men but as warriors. "Now, if you see my girl here on the streets,
you protect her," he said.

Their transformation was immediate and visible. Now warriors, their backs straightening, "We'll look out after your girl,
Doctor."

Tsehai's comments on Mandaza's comments on George's
dream are worth relating.

> The dreamer doesn't know he's being recruited into the position
> of being a warrior and a healer. Mandaza's interpretation shifts
> everything. The spirits send you the dream not because you're
> the biggest victim but because you have the power to carry the
> burden of awareness in a violent situation. Spirit is trying to re-
> veal to you that you are not a victim, you are the family war-
> rior. This is very important because African-Americans often see
> themselves as profound victims. These witch spirits, the spirits
> of deception, come in and say, "Oh, this is easy. I don't have to
> do much except make sure this little warrior doesn't recognize
> himself and thinks, Oh, poor me."

In Bantu culture self-recognition means recognition of the
presence of the ancestors, the spirits of protection.
Turning white is a particular kind of soul-eating. Since whiteness is rewarded in America as a matter of course, it should
not be surprising that blacks are susceptible to the witches that
want to whiten them.

Tommy Walters was a strange man with a strange life.
Because I was homeless myself a long time ago, I feel a certain
comradery with the homeless. They remind me of things that I
believe I shouldn't forget.

I took Tommy out for a couple of Big Macs and a shake.
HIV positive, a drug addict, a born again Christian, blue-black
complexion, he admitted freely that he much preferred white
people over blacks, who he claimed treated homeless people
with contempt. Michael Jackson was a role model for him, and

he'd sometimes make a pilgrimage to a supermarket that was near Jackson's house to fondle the fruit that the singer himself might have touched.

> In my dream there was a side of this town where only black people lived and died. The houses were in poor shape, the food was scarce, and it was a violent place to live. Me and a group of friends played near a wooded area which separated the white people from the area where we lived.
>
> The whites would come and hire blacks to work for them. There were often a lot of fights between blacks to get into the white men's trucks to work. I remember seeing men and women die for lack of work or food. Also the white people would often kill blacks who refused to return to where they were supposed to live.
>
> I was lucky one day, and a white man hired me to clean up his yard. I was fifteen years old and had a bright mind. The white man liked me because I could read and write and I knew the Bible.
>
> Every day I'd go off in a deep section of the wooded area and watch for this white man's car. He would appear in the dark of night in a white car emerging from a bright light. As I got inside the car, the light would go out, and the car would seem to disappear and then reappear in the white part of town.
>
> The white man was a doctor and gave me some medicine. I'd lay down upon his bed and put my head in his wife's lap, and she'd stroke my hair. This I did for seven days until the last time I laid down. I woke up in a vision, and my skin was white. I grew up to marry the doctor's daughter and keep his name like I was his son. We were all very happy together, and I never returned to the black side of town again. This dream was very real to me.

Mandaza found this dream especially provocative and talked about it at length. The incentives to "turn white" are alive and well in Zimbabwe also even though the country has only a one percent white minority. For Mandaza the overweaning efforts to become white divide the community from its ancestors and therefore invite chaos. On a more personal level, it means that ngangas like himself are regarded as backward and superstitious by a growing number of upwardly mobile Africans.

> This is a very powerful dream, and if this man doesn't find a way back to his spirits, he will surely die.
>
> This is the way it is. They take young Africans and educate them so that they forget completely about their people and become white. Africans are told, 'We are taking you to America. You will become a doctor. You will become a preacher. And you will return back and destroy African people.' I'm talking about people who go to America and come back with white souls. Or they go to Russia, and they come back and tell you that Russian is the only language, that the Russian way of living is better. Our own culture is being destroyed by Western culture because the West tells us that Africa is very primitive, very superstitious. When these ones with white souls return, they say, 'I am educated. I am civilized. I no longer eat sadza with my own hands.' Colonialism sets it up so that people long to be white because white is supposed to mean intelligence, peace, richness. I will never get any support from such a person.
>
> The white doctor who takes him in is really a witch. Look at the time he was taken: lights off so he does not see. What did you say? That this dreamer uses heroin? Look at this: The doctor gives him poison like a witch that transforms him into a white man so he is now a part of the system. This is witchcraft, the kind that attacks the community as a whole. One joins the system which is destructive, which is evil in the eyes of the Creator.
>
> In such a dream the spirits of witches are masquerading as water spirits and saying, "Come to my house. You will be happy. Marry my daughter," and then those witches eat the soul.

In TWIN OF ANOTHER TRIBE I tell Mandaza,

> [that he has] returned me to a medical way of knowing that perceives the circles within the circles within the circles: self, family, clan and tribe encircled by the ancestors; the ancestors encircled by the elemental intelligences of earth, fire, water and air; and all of it encircled by the endless presence of God. It seems

to me that Bantu medicine is about reconciliation within a field of relationships.

I call this field of relationships the village of the ancestors, the living and the unborn. In these pages you have met a few of the living who inhabit this village. This village could well be in Africa, but as it turns out, this is America. Perhaps you recognize these people, or maybe they just remind you of somebody else: Andrea, bleary-eyed from a long night of studying; Tamika, sweet and fragile, anticipating the birth of her first child; Nikki, bright eyed and idealistic and so passionate about acting; Mr. Cary, in and out of prison, in and out; eleven-year-old George who knows nothing of prison and is so scared for his little brother; and Tommy, the madman in the ragged clothes fondling nectarines at the supermarket and wishing he were Michael Jackson. Perhaps you recognize these ones, and perhaps you also see that you yourself live in the village of the ancestors, the living and the unborn.

The European equivalent of soul eaters would probably be vampires, those who suck the vitality from the living to aggrandize themselves, to extend their lives and grow fat at the expense of others. In Africa nightmares are often attributed to soul eaters, especially nightmares of being pursued, captured, pinned down, confined, sometimes even eaten. Soul-eating has been a consistent way Africans have tried to understand the way white folks act since the Portuguese first made contact with the kingdom of the Kongo in 1487. Throughout West and Central Africa, slavery, colonialism and apartheid have consistently been understood as organized and systematic forms of soul-eating. In America, on the level of the dream, racism is understood in exactly the same fashion.

Systematic soul-eating was unknown in Africa before the advent of slavery. Most traditional cultures have stories about witches. In Africa the witch was often a member of your family — an uncle perhaps — who out of spite or envy found his way under your skin and was undermining your life. Witchcraft was a way to make sense out of the craziness that can happen in an extended family in the village. It required slavery for Bantu people to create a new sociological category: the witch who is a white stranger, who eats soul in an organized way, who one has no intimate ties with, who is often anonymous and quite out of control, often someone who one must work for in order to survive.

Bantu medicine is about reconciliation within a field of relationship, but it's also about the movement of Spirit. In some respects it's like Chinese medicine which seeks to unblock chi, the life force, so it flows unimpeded through the body. But for Bantu people the "body" is not only the individual's flesh and blood, it is the village as well. Witchcraft is one way the flow of spirit is blocked, the soul of the individual or of the community is bottled up. Witchcraft not only messes with relationships within the community, its most dreadful effect is that it can impede one's relationship to God.

Or as the psalmist David said when he was in captivity in Babylon,

> By the rivers of Babylon we sat and wept when we remembered Zion. There on the poplars we hung our harps, for there our captors asked us for songs. Our tormentors demanded songs of joy; they said, "Sing us one of the songs of Zion."
>
> How can we sing the songs of the Lord while in a foreign land?

5

IMPRISONED IN SOMEONE ELSE'S DREAM

Back in the 1970's when Joseph Boskin, a professor of history and African American studies at Boston University, was researching American humor, he came across this joke:

> Way down South in slavery times, there was a handsome fella, a muscular young slave. One night he found himself stumbling out of bed like a sleepwalker. He slid out the door and walked half-naked through the cotton field to the master's house. When he got to the big white house, he went inside, straight up the stairs to where the master's young daughter's room was.
>
> Now, when he was walking up the stairs, she woke right up, and when he opened her bedroom door, she was so scared she couldn't talk or scream or anything. He lifted her up in his bare arms kind of roughlike and took her out to the edge of the cotton field, trembling, all helpless and everything; and he stood still above her, looking real powerful with the moon shining all over his muscles. When he bent down and ripped off her nightgown, she asked, real scared, "Are y'all going to rape me?"
>
> He looked in her eyes and said, "You tell me, Missy. It's your dream."

It's your dream. Your dream. Being fixed, worked on, hoodooed in both Africa and among the diaspora is sometimes understood as having one's soul bound or bottled up. It is a matter of being imprisoned within somebody else's dream. Consequently, when it comes to the witchcraft of racism, the

76

stakes are very high. One must both extricate oneself from white fantasy and discover and explore an authentic self, or one will be consumed by a white nightmare.

Witchcraft can always be done ritually, but given the vast job of suppressing and exploiting hundreds of millions of people, ritual hoodoo is quite inefficient. It is both inefficient and completely unnecessary. White supremacy, after all, controls the parameters of the dream that we live in, from the economy to the media, from the logic with which we think and interpret things to what we are taught in school.

I understand witchcraft from three angles: that of having been a witch, having been hoodooed myself and having ritually intervened as a nganga in Africa and America with patients who have been "worked."

Among Bantu people the ideal is to walk the middle path between duty and desire. In Kongo culture ndoki, the passions of individualism, of the intent to draw power to oneself for the sake of being effective in the world, is considered an essential and necessary aspect of human nature. And yet witches are called bandoki because they have amplified this individualism to the point of breaking rank with the reciprocities of community life. They have become hungry, greedy. Power has become their drug of choice. The U.N. informs us that the 225 wealthiest people control the equivalent income of the two and a half billion poorest. I remember watching Oliver Stone's movie WALL STREET about that particular world of white male sociopaths "looking out for number one." In Bantu Africa they say that those who eat souls gather in small circles in the forest out of sight of the village, and in these circles they reinforce each others' values, each others' greed so that it takes on a semblance of being normal. To be a witch among witches, the initiation requires that you first eat the soul of your kin. As in Africa, so in America, the threshold is crossed when the wife, the children, one's parents are sacrificed for ambition.

In an unpublished book, CAPABLE OF SUCH BEAUTY (about white people's dreams about black people), I write of my own crossing over the River Jordan that preceded my being initiated by Mandaza. Although this crossing lasted four years, the final eight months were bitter beyond telling for it was during that time that the spirit of the witch had to be crushed, when I had to call on my own spirits to undo certain qualities that, though I had lied about them, I had also come to mistake for myself.

If I had to name the spirit of the witch in psychological language, it would be narcissistic self-intent coupled with a kind of ambition that makes a genuine and true sense that others exist, that they are as real and vivid as one's self, ultimately irrelevant. Others may exist as allies in pursuing one's desires or as the objects of desire, but the give and take of true relationship threatens the witch spirit and must be avoided at all costs.

Take, for example, Donald Trump's account of his daily life:

> I wake up most mornings very early and spend the first hour or so each day reading the morning newspapers. I usually arrive at my office by nine and get on the phone. There's rarely a day with fewer than fifty calls, and often it runs to over a hundred. In between I have at least a dozen meetings. The majority occur on the spur of the moment, and few of them last longer than fifteen minutes. I rarely stop for lunch. I leave my office by six-thirty, but I frequently make calls from home until midnight, and all weekend long . . . It never stops and I wouldn't have it any other way. I don't do it for the money. I've got enough, much more than I'll ever need. I do it to do it.

This naked, blind self-intent has nothing to do with race per se; it is rampant in Africa, especially as traditional culture breaks down and ndoki becomes less and less tempered by the values of sustaining the village. But for white people the breakdown of tradition, rather, the transformation of tradition began with the rise of Protestantism and capitalism. Traditional village life in Europe was remarkably similar to that in Africa, its definitions of witchcraft (vampirism) very much the same as well as its emphasis on maintaining community; improvement of one's lot was always to be weighed within the context of community welfare. With the birth of Protestantism and capitalism, coinciding, it should be noted, with the trans-Atlantic slave trade, traditional European values were turned completely inside out. What had been regarded as vice or at the least human frailty — the pull to self-aggrandizement — was now understood as economic virtue. Ndoki, the "natural frailty" that is so necessary to human ambition but which can become unrestrained witchcraft, was transformed into the essential virtue that "makes the world go round." What was once called a witch is now called a "real go-getter." Should hundreds of millions of lives be destroyed in all this go-getting? Well, you can't make an omelet without breaking a few eggs.

To extend a metaphor, dreams of soul-eating are dreams of being broken open so someone can eat an omelet: The breaking up of those fields of relationship within which the soul thrives and Spirit moves. Soul-eating assaults those elemental and necessary worlds of meaning that people of African descent have relied on for millennia to make sense of their lives.

"You tell me, Missy. It's your dream."

I remember once watching one of the ordinary dreams — one of the ordinary dramas — of soul-eating unfold at the hospital. I tried to intervene but don't think I was especially effective.

It was a rather slow shift, and I was actually engrossed in reading a book about apartheid when just down the hallway, I witnessed a brief confrontation. Indeed, had I not been reading this book, I might well not have noticed or made much of what came down; so small, ordinary and typical it was.

Apparently Wendy, a black nurses' aide, had accidentally emptied a patient's urinal into the toilet instead of adding the urine to a 24-hour specimen container that was to be sent to the lab. Nora, the white nurse she worked with, stood in front of her, her face not six inches from Wendy's, and read her the riot act in full public view. Wendy took it all in silently. That was the extent of it: soul-eating in America.

I quietly took Wendy aside, just to say that I witnessed it, that no one should treat another human being that way. I chose not to speak of the racial dynamic because I didn't want to force an interpretation that might not have been her own.

I also talked to Nora. Not wanting to animate defensiveness, I addressed the racial issue very gently, suggesting that although I knew she hadn't meant it that way, there were good reasons why it appeared to be a "black/white thing."

Dialogue quickly becomes incoherent when two people don't share the same language. Nora expressed how tired she was of black people being so paranoid. "All this talk of racism is a bunch of nonsense. Just look at the talk shows on TV. They all agree with me."

Who am I to question the wisdom of talk shows? I don't even own a damn television. I was getting angry, and so I disengaged into a familiar sense of hopelessness.

In the Kongo they say, "Although witches recognize one another, no witch can admit to himself that he is one." Within narcissistic self-intent one is very nearly blind to the fact that otherness exists and therefore blind to the damage caused by one's actions. In the Bantu world it is a given that many acts of witchcraft are performed unconsciously. "When you act without knowing what you are doing," says Mandaza, "it means you are possessed by a spirit. It happens all the time in the world. Yes, racism is a good example of that one. But it happens in so many ways. The spirits can cause a lot of trouble because people act strongly when they're possessed. They are caught next door doing things, and they don't even know why or what they were doing. They are reported to the local kraalhead. The case is tried. In court the person will say, 'I don't even know what I was doing. I don't even know that I was here at this house.' Racism works like that too."

Nora taught me something essential about soul-eating. I do not believe she is "racist" in the way the word is usually used in America. I've watched her with coworkers and witnessed an easy and spontaneous warmth with black nurses who share her social status; and needless to say, she would never have talked to a "superior" of any race the way she talked to Wendy. Witchcraft moves along a gradient of power. It preys on those of lower status. On one hand it is clear the witch spirit seeks to debilitate and weaken but where the gradient of power is already established by institutional hierarchy (such as that in a modern hospital or in a racist society), souls are to be had for the eating. For a witch, hierarchy is a moveable feast, and since hierarchy is profoundly a racial matter in America, it is the souls of people of color that awaken the witch's hunger for power. To put it simply, racism doesn't require that one have bad thoughts or feelings about people of color. The system relies on something much subtler and much more pervasive: the unconsciousness with which one serves the spirit of hierarchy, the degree to which one's identity depends on unconsciously living out dramas of power and powerlessness, master and slave.

A few months after I witnessed this interaction, Wendy offered me the following dream about Nora:

> I'd just fallen asleep, and I felt suffocated. I opened my eyes, and Nora was right in front of my face, except she was a cat with Nora's face! The cat tried to scratch my eyes out. I always wondered about that witch and her damned cats. That's all she ever talks about — her cats.

Mandaza says,

> This woman is suffering from proper witchcraft. In this dream, the witch is not trying to eat the soul; it is trying to scratch her eyes out so that she can't perceive the evil that is happening.

Wendy's dream partakes of a theme that is common in both Africa and America — the alliance between witches and certain animals. Compare, for example, a dream collected by another Michael Jackson (not the pop singer) during his fieldwork in Sierra Leone among the Kuranko. His informant, Morowa, had lost several children due to witchcraft. After the witch died, he was haunted by her spirit.

"As he slept, it settled on his head. He opened his eyes but could not cry out. He lay in terror as though an immense weight were pressing down on him." Eventually the witch's spirit was caught in the form of a lizard. Jackson comments that "animals most commonly associated with witches — palmbirds, lizards, toads, snakes, cats, vultures, owls — are also structurally ambiguous. They are of the wild yet often enter and live within the village."

In African village life, as in the rural American South, a semipermeable boundary exists between the realm of the wild and the habitation of people. Ancestor spirits live in the wild as animals — for example, Mandaza's totem the lion. I call the female elephant 'mother' because she embodies the Mambokadzi who has received me as one of her children. But the forest is also the realm of people and spirits one has not relationship to, the ngozi or enraged dead, predator animals and evil sorcerers. In the dreams of African people on both sides of the Atlantic, whites often appear as creatures of the bush who invade the realm of the village as per above: foreigners, monstrous spirits, predatory animals, evil sorcerers and the enraged dead (ngozi). Wendy dreamt her coworker as what in South Carolina is called a wampus-cat (from the Bantu wapampas, "Be troubled! Be afraid!"). In other words, Wendy's dream soul recognized that Nora was acting in a way that violated the rules of civility, the etiquette of village life that depends on reciprocity: She was inviting into the village a wildness that belongs to the bush.

Take, for example, these dreams given to me by Mr. Cary:

> These white people was riding around on these giant ants catching me, but I would always escape, and they would find me and make the ants bite me on my butt and head.

> There was these big white chickens eating black people up and then spitting them back out and eating them over and over. I started to cry because I didn't want to be eaten.

"The ants are white witches," says Mandaza.

> This is slavery again, white soldiers looking for him, capturing
> him. They say, 'Hunt for that one; he has escaped. Bring him
> back alive.' The spirit of this man is very powerful. They could
> arrest this person, put him in jail, and tomorrow morning he is
> not there. The spirit of our prophet Chaminuka was very much
> like this one.
>
> But this other dream of his is quite different though it is also
> a dream of witchcraft. Some people have the power to attack
> others by turning into different animals. The spirits are saying,
> "We will protect our son. We don't want him to be eaten at all,"
> which means that this man requires initiation so his spirits can
> protect him.

The bleakest dream of this sort was given to me by Terrence
Taylor, a young man in his mid twenties who works in a photo-
copy place in West Los Angeles. Terrence was studying the "rap-
ture," when, according to born-again Christians, the saved are
transported into heaven just before the reign of the Anti-Christ,
the "Beast."

> I woke up and found that there were only black people left in
> the world. All the nice houses were gone too. I walked around
> for a while. All the black folks were stunned and speechless.
> Then this giant white scorpion tried to chase me. I ran back to
> my apartment, and its tail broke through the window and tried
> to sting me.

"Strange," said Terrence, "No blacks in heaven, I guess."

"This is a very profound dream when I look at it," says
Mandaza.

> God is saying don't look at the color of a person. Let us look at
> everyone as if they were just one heart, one mind. This monster,
> this Anti-Christ says there must be white, there must be black. It
> is like a devil who is lying to him, who is saying, "You are left be-
> hind. Look at why. You are black." The devil is saying only whites
> are allowed in heaven and blacks remain behind in poverty and
> are tortured.

Some racists call blacks "animals," but in my examination of nearly two hundred racial dreams of white people about blacks, the dream connection between blacks and animals is quite rare. And although Africans have long been associated with cannibalism in the white imagination, on the level of the dream, I've yet to find any black cannibals. Among Africans and African-Americans dreamers, however, white cannibals are a not uncommon theme. Alice Walker touches on this in THE TEMPLE OF MY FAMILIAR.

> "What do you think of white people?" asked Robin's voice . . . .
>
> "I'm afraid of them," was her reply.
>
> "When you look at them," said the voice, "how do they look to you?"
>
> "Very fat," she said. "They are always eating, eating, eating. Everywhere you go they are sitting down eating. In Paris, they are eating. In London, they are eating. In Rome, they eat and eat. It makes me feel afraid."
>
> "Why do you feel afraid?"
>
> "When I see them eating, I feel myself to be very hungry. Skin and bones. And I feel their teeth on my leg. But when I look down it is not their teeth, only a chain. I think that when they called us 'cannibals' they were projecting."

America, says the Vietnamese Buddhist master Thich Nhat Hanh, is a land of hungry ghosts. In Central Africa his insight would be translated into the idiom of witchcraft: eating others but ultimately eating away at one's own soul as well.

Walker continues: "Sometimes I see myself joining them at the table and I'm eating, eating, eating too." But the self remains, "as poor and emaciated as ever. She and her babies. Nothing but eyes and skin and bone. And I'm afraid, because I love her so very much, and she is the self I have lost."

White witches riding ants, biting; chickens eating up blacks, spitting them out. Consider Larry Parker's dream. Larry is a forty-five-year-old social worker from Phoenix, Arizona.

These Chinese and white people are eating blacks in a kind of chop suey.

Or Veronica Sawyer, a co-worker, dreamed when she was a little girl,

I was at my grandfather's house, and he was cooking breakfast. I saw these filthy white people, smaller than dwarfs and buck ugly climb out the bushes next to the house and climb through the windows. I hid in a closet and watched through a crack. One of them took a spatula and cut my grandfather's fingers off and ate them like sausages.

Or Zora, one of the twins I mentioned in Chapter 2, she remembers this recurring dream from when she was five or six years old.

I was in the forest behind a tree. I couldn't tell if it was day or night. A beautiful white man was looking in my direction, but I don't think he saw me. He was beautifully dressed and had a kind of magnetism to him and was surrounded by beautiful white ladies wearing lingerie. I was real scared, but there was a kind of euphoria with the women, and I wanted to be one of them.

The ladies came from out of the woods and went in a barn, and they circled around him. I went in, too, but was terrified and hid in a hay loft.

He turned around and saw me. His eyes were red, and I knew he was a vampire, and he floated off the ground and started coming to me. His teeth were sharp and white, and I'd wake up in mortal terror.

"This is proper witchcraft here, nothing other than witchcraft," says Mandaza.

Look at those eyes that pin that little girl down so they can suck the blood out of her! And those witches that come out of the bush. That house is completely unprotected. This one here is quite an evil something back in those days of slavery.

If someone came to me with these dreams, I would do very strong initiation, calling their spirits back into their body for protection.

When I first met Mandaza, what most impressed me was how he walks through the world — of course his generosity and poise but also his actual gait: confident and solid and yet without arrogance as if he trusted the earth to uphold him and was grateful for it. I would walk behind him watching and wondering how it would feel to move in such a fashion. Later when our friendship deepened, I gained insight into his experience of moving through the world, his constant knowledge that he does not walk alone: since initiation, his spirits lead him, protect him, ease his path.

"Whenever I go into Bulawayo," he once told me, "my spirits accompany me, protect me, help me out so that I feel quite safe in the world. I walk into a store, for example, but my spirits go in before I do to see what is happening there. Warrior spirits move in to make sure I am safe; and the njuzu, the water spirits, the peacemakers — they make everything very smooth, very quiet actually. And my spirits follow behind me as well so I am not attacked from the back."

In the last chapter I mentioned that Bantu medicine sees human life as existing within concentric circles — self, family, kin, village, tribe — all contained within the boundless grace of God. For that reason among many Bantu people, the ancestors are called forth to inspirit mojo for protection of the various bounded worlds we live in. (Let me say in passing that those who find this primitive or superstitious might recall that Catholic priests perform the same act when they call down the body and blood of Christ into bread and wine.) This mojo is placed under a bed, for example, to protect the soul from being attacked during sleep when he or she is most vulnerable. In the American South, the bed was sometimes encircled by a boundary of red pepper to keep witches and haints at bay. The mojo was also often buried under the doorway to protect the house or worn beneath clothing so that the ancestors accompanied one as one went about the business of the world. Robert Farris Thompson says the Bakongo custom of wearing a round shell around the neck to protect the roundness of the soul from predatory witches has its equivalent in the American South — pennies in the shoe. To the best of my knowledge, the Bantu practice of burying mojo at the edge of the village never made its way to America.

Fu Kiau Bunseki and Thompson found that the poetic sensibility with which mojo is crafted is virtually the same on both sides of the Atlantic. Thompson writes,

> There are anti-hex roots galore throughout black America today that are usually wrapped in red flannel "so nobody can put evil on you — if they do, it will turn to them." To the Bakongo these American charms appear to derive from minkisi, wambi and minkisi wa nsisi — danger minkisi — which are contained in crimson cloth.

It must be understood that both traditional Bantu people and African-Americans have a deeply ambivalent attitude towards mojo/nkisi, an attitude that is rooted in the way of the water spirits. Put simply, mojo could be used for good or evil. Those who veer away from solidarity with the community, witches, have long used mojo as a way of enslaving the ancestors for selfish ends. Does one serve the ancestors, or does one coerce the ancestors to serve egotism? For this reason water spirit priests were often at odds with ngangas involved in the making of mojo/nkisi. This split also survived intact in America: the Christian parson carries the same role and sensibility of a priest of the water spirits. The root doctor, both in Africa and the American South, may heal but is also often skilled in hexing. One finds this split played out in a thousand ways among African-Americans, the ethics of the old spirituals and gospel music being quite different than that of jazz or the blues. Whereas the old spirituals sang of returning home, the urban blues, which pioneered a new understanding of black individualism, sang of exile: "Sometimes I feel like a motherless child."

I had brought mojo with me during my first trip to Africa, a leather bag gathering the protective presence of my community: a gold leaf from my daughter, a piece of amethyst from my friend Amanda, a vial of sacred oil strained from the body of a

Tibetan holy man, fragrant herbs, a few lines of poetry. During my initiation Mandaza assured me that I didn't need my mojo for protection anymore. "But you can use it for healing." Just as St. Paul speaks of the body as the temple of the Holy Spirit, the Shona see it as the house of the ancestors. The body is the mojo, and so one moves through the world with confidence and grace as long as one sticks close to the way of the spirits that inhabit one's life.

The ethical question so essential to the Bantu world, how to walk in balance between duty and desire, has been made fierce with the Great Migration of black Americans from the rural South to urban America. Scarcely fifty years had passed after the end of the greatest forced immigration in human history when black Americans set off on one of the most massive voluntary migrations in human history. Roughly six and a half million people moved from the countryside to the city between 1910 and 1970. There was no precedence for this among an African people though rapid urbanization is very much a reality in the Motherland. Black Americans are without question the avant garde. It has been the burden of African Americans to reinvent African culture to come to terms with the big city. Duty, desire and spiritual protection in a dangerous world are interrelated concerns for all African people. Much of the cultural plurality of contemporary black life is about the various strategies and experiments of keeping faith with those traditional concerns in environments that are often extremely overwhelming.

The water spirit priest and the maker of nkisi; the parson and the root doctor; gospel music and urban blues; Sister Rosetta Tharpe on one hand and on the other Ralph Ellison's bluesman Jim Trueblood; Martin Luther King and his dream and Malcolm who spoke of protecting the community by whatever means necessary — again. In Africa, it is said, all things are doubled.

Likewise in America.

6

SOME DEAD NEGRO'S GRIEF

"124 was spiteful. Full of a baby's venom," begins Morrison's
BELOVED.

> For years each put up with the spite in his own way, but by 1873
> Sethe and her daughter Denver were its only victims . . . . Who
> would have thought that a little old baby could harbor such
> rage? Rutting among the stones under the eyes of the engraver's
> son was not enough.

Sethe had to "live out her years in a house palsied by the baby's
fury at having its throat cut."

When Sethe suggests to her mother-in-law Baby Suggs that
perhaps they should move, she responds,

> What'd be the point? Not a house in the country ain't padded to
> the rafters with some dead Negro's grief. We lucky this ghost is
> a baby. My husband's spirit was to come back in here? Or yours?
> Don't talk to me. You lucky.

Some dead negro's grief — and fury. Or rather, fury first and
then grief. Hard, sometimes, to get to the grief that these spirits
carry, the spirits of those cut down by violence, the ones that in
Shona are called ngozi.

I once submitted to the dreary task of collating statistics on
black violence against other black people in America, which for
the most part means young men killing other young men. In another context, say Vietnam, this would be called a "body count."
I wanted to make a broad rhetorical statement comparing the

body count between Malcolm's assassination in 1965 and the murder of his widow, thirty-three years later burned to death by their eleven-year-old grandson, to the number of slaves imported from Bantu Africa during the trade. Or measure it against the fate of those other "dead negros," 1,100 of them strung up by the Klan over a century of terror. Or against the mere 55,000 American dead in Southeast Asia over a comparable period. Mercifully, I lost my notes, but I recall that the number approached 200,000. In the face of such a number, rhetoric becomes ash, and cleverness dishonors the fallen.

In Bantu Africa, the plague of ngozi is understood as a medical problem of terrifying proportions because the slain come back to torment the living, bring nightmares, kill children, drive people mad, and inspire further violence, generating even more ngozi.

As one of Morrison's characters says, "You know as well as I do that people who die bad don't stay in the ground."

Ngozi do not merely torment those who have shed blood. Until the spirit is dealt with, it will move through the family line, sometimes for generations. Mandaza has noted that whites are very often haunted by the spirits of dead slaves and that these spirits accompany them and distort their lives. "The sins of the fathers are visited upon the children."

The spirits of those killed in the war against apartheid, the twenty thousand Ndebele slain by their Shona compatriots after white supremacy was defeated, the violence of poverty that persists in the townships — Mandaza's work is inevitably deeply involved in chasing away ngozi. The work of dealing with ngozi relies on the subtlest and most complex skills of the ngangas' craft — the fierceness of the warrior who protects the afflicted and the tenderness of the peacemaker before a spirit that is justly enraged.

> The ngozi are very dangerous. They are the most dangerous spirits. For example, I'm mad at my own wife. The ngozi speaks through me, making her the enemy. "Why did you kill me? I'm

going to revenge." You may hear voices in your house or in your head. You may run away from your home and say, "I cannot sleep here. Something terrible is going on in this house." That is how ngozi act.

It is a terrible thing, really, to kill another person. So you need to actually listen to what that ngozi wants you to do so that it will leave you in peace. It may tell you that it wants so many head of cattle to be taken to its home, given to its family.

In a sense they are not evil. They just want us to come to terms with them. What they want is justice. But they become evil because we refuse to look at what we've done or what our kin or ancestors have done.

Bantu medicine is about the free movement of Spirit through the village. Illness of all kinds — physical, mental, spiritual, social — is caused when the spirit is blocked. Witchcraft is one way of impeding with the movement of Spirit, but so is the presence of ngozi among us and our refusal to come to terms with them. Mandaza routinely uses the word "obstacle" interchangeably with "ngozi" and once summarized his way of healing and initiation as just removing the obstacle, after which "the Spirit just comes in and does all the work."

The medical understanding of ngozi as obstacle is reflected in traditional Greek medicine as well. The pre-Christian understanding of the "diabolic" is somewhat similar to the Shona understanding of ngozi. The Greek word "diabolos" means literally "to throw across, to impede" and is related to the word "slanderer" — thus the theological idea that the Devil is the father of lies. A cluster of ideas is shared between Europe and Africa: To the degree that we lie about what we do, we are ensnared by the diabolic. We risk being either or both victims of the diabolical and vehicles for it to vent its fury on the world until we look that fury in the eye. In either case, whether we are victims, victimizers or both, the diabolic, the ngozi remains as one of the primary obstacles that keeps Spirit from moving in the world in the way that it desires.

"In dreams," says Mandaza, "ngozi can take on any form. They put on masks. He may appear in the form of my grandfather, but he is after me to kill me. He disguises himself as a good spirit trying to get closer to me. Sometimes they put on the mask of a white man. How do I know that this white man in my dream is a ngozi? He chases me around. He wants to do something evil, to hit me, to kill me. He is always cursing at me. Ngozi not only disguise themselves as white men — any race, really. Blacks as well. Ngozi are very clever, and they will seek out the form that most frightens you. If you are afraid of dogs, ngozi will take the form of a dog. But with blacks, white ngozi are very common."

Consider, for example, the dream of Carlos Delgado. Carlos is an Afro-Cuban man living in the Los Angeles area.

> I was being chased around my house by my father, but he had horns like the devil. He had two white thugs with him, and he shouted to them, "Get that nigger," and they went after me.

Mandaza says,

> The ngozi is disguising itself as his father. He is like the king who controls these white spirits; so we must separate out the good spirits in this man from ngozi so they can protect him.

In this dream it is clear how ngozi shapeshift into images of terror: the face of the murderous father with horns, the black devil who calls his own son "nigger," his white allies. From a strictly Bantu perspective, dreams of ngozi, even white ngozi are not racial dreams. The "father" in this dream is neither a "black man" nor a "father" with horns; he is an enraged and dangerous spirit who is quite skilled at reading Carlos's fear and then embodying it. Neither are the white thugs "white people," but because of the ancient recognition that whites eat souls, it cannot be surprising that ngozi exploit the black terror of the white witch. Mandaza has pointed out to me that ngozi in the dreams of whites are often black, but he has had to remind me repeatedly that they are not black people at all but spirits who are knowledgeable about what frightens whites. In other words, ngozi use the madness of racial history and racial mythology as raw material to create the perfect nightmare.

There are two factors that make this even more complicated, that in fact allow this nightmare to seep into our waking lives and shape it.

Firstly, such spirits do possess people, as Mandaza explained in his example of a ngozi overtaking him so that he is, for no clear reason, suddenly enraged at his wife. Much white bigotry can be understood as whites taken by such spirits as is quite evident, say, when one looks at old photos of white citizens taunting black children in the struggles for integration: the mask frozen, grotesque and quite obviously not human.

Secondly, white folks look spooky, and so blacks are given to projecting onto whites the figure of the ghost. I've collected numerous stories from blacks and whites about their first childhood impressions of the racial other, and one theme that recurs is that the other is a "spook," not really human, from another incomprehensible world quite beyond the familiar world of friends and kin. The shock of simple human difference cannot be underestimated. If those who look spooky have power over you and are unkind and one is not really able to protect oneself from them, the ghostlikeness of the other will be understood as malevolent, and I dare say, not only humanly malevolent but spiritually dangerous.

This hallucinatory and mutually reinforcing dream of interracial spookiness is underscored by Clarence Major's dictionary on black American slang, JUBA TO JIVE:

> Spook n. (1800s-1960s). Originally used by black slaves as a reference to ghosts and later as a reference to white people as "ghost-like." A black person, a negro, picked up from derogatory white use and used ironically.

Actual white spookiness, whites possessed by spooks, spookiness projected onto whites, being without spiritual protection in a world that is downright spooky — none of this exactly has anything to do with ngozi except to note that they have tapped into complex interracial feedback patterns to conjure up what amounts to abject psychological terror in blacks. In other words, the soul is trapped in a hall of mirrors between white people who look and sometimes act like ngozi and ngozi who masquerade as white people. Anxiety and the paralysis of will in both waking life and sleep are not uncommon. Spirit is blocked off from two directions: the reality of racism and the fear of ngozi projected onto whites, giving them even more power than they already have.

All this being said, it is critical that when working with ngozi, they be recognized as merely ngozi, whatever shape they happen to take. To do otherwise is to succumb to even more powerlessness within the nightmare of racism.

Mary Jamison, an eleven-year-old girl from Biloxi, Mississippi had a recurring ngozi dream. Her mother sent it to me after having read an article I'd written about racial dreaming.

> I was being chased by a white doctor wearing a white coat, and he had this needle, I mean really big, and he was going to stick me with it. He chased me to the edge of a cliff. I always wake up then because I can't escape.

Mandaza comments,

> The ancestors were overpowered by this ngozi. That is why they are showing her this dream, to show her they are powerless to defend her.
>
> It is this spirit that is shutting her outside of the community, making sure everything goes wrong, that she is vulnerable to being attacked.
>
> This kind of ngozi moves from person to person in the same family or even different families. If it comes to Michael's home and doesn't find a strong spirit to protect you, it will come in and use you, but if it finds that you have been properly initiated and your spirits are protecting you, it won't come into your home at all. If there are loopholes in the dreamer, it will enter.
>
> Biloxi, Mississippi has a ngozi. That much is clear. There is a ngozi in the village, and its intention is to cause death by what-

ever means. If someone came to me like this, I'd use my herbs and chase that spirit away.

Luanne Baker, a nurse and co-worker dreamt,

> I was being chased by a white man at a public park, and I ran into the bathroom. He broke down the door of the stall and was going to rape me. I was completely cornered.

"Luanne's spirit is defenseless," says Mandaza. "It has no power to defend itself. Yes! Ngozi rape people like that. She needs somebody to initiate her so she can stand on her own two feet."

I am struck that Mary and Luanne share the same dream. A child's fears, a woman's fears — the white doctor's needle; the white rapist's phallus; both pursued, cornered, unprotected, nailed to the place where violation seems inevitable; paralyzed with fear.

The theme of running from ngozi is very common. Not surprisingly, even among law-abiding blacks, the ngozi take the form of white policemen. Art Patterson, my Pentecostal friend, had this dream in his late twenties:

> Nelson Mandela was elected leader over black affairs in the United States, but an evil white dictator was coming to take over. On a hill near my house in Venice, I saw two white men with guns chasing black people. They were somehow connected with this dictator. Even though I was at a distance, they saw me and started to chase me. The police also got involved. Most of the dream was about getting away from them. It was exciting; it was like I was sonic or something. There were some close calls, but they still couldn't catch me.

Mandaza was very impressed by Art's dream:

> This is what it is like when you are initiated. Those spirits will never catch up with him. He is well protected. His spirits are very powerful. There are times to fight back, and other times to escape. The warrior spirits know when to do either. This trickster spirit says, "If I fight those people, I'm just wasting my time." Trickster spirits run fast. They can get away from anything.

Brer Rabbit, High John the Conqueror, Legba, the Akan spi-der trickster Ananse (who in Louisiana was called Aunt Nancy) — there are reasons that trickster stories have been preserved and retold and apparently reinvented in the dreams of black Americans. Recall that in the last chapter I wrote of the witch-craft of racism as being stranded in someone else's dream — the tangled net of "their" agendas, definitions, fantasies, the person with the quick feet, quick tongue and quick mind is one who would slide lithely through the net.

Art's dream stands parallel to Charles Jefferson's, a com-munity activist in South Central L.A. Charles dreamt this dream when he was in the merchant marines in his early thirties and had to share a trans-Atlantic voyage with a bigot who "was al-ways in my face." In the dream the man was again in his face, and Charles shouted, "Get away from me. I'm a man. Treat me like a man or get out of here," and the spirit fled. That morning over breakfast Charles was able to reenact his dream to great effect. His tormentor began keeping a respectful distance.

Like Art, Mandaza recognized Charles as someone who was acting like an initiated man, deeply rooted in the authority to chase off ngozi.

> That dreamer has a warrior spirit who can face any situation. He saw the ngozi that possessed this white man, and he sent it away. That is what I do as a nganga.

For the Shona the most powerful allies for working with ngozi are the white and black Chapungu. The white Chapungu, the fish eagle, is regal and intelligent in the arts of peacemak-ing. The black eagle is the fiercest of warriors who withholds nothing in defense of those who cannot defend themselves. "the white eagle in king and the black is prime minister", says Mandaza. The way of the warrior must obey the way of the peacemaker. Without this collaboration the peacemakers skill would have no edge, would be ineffectual and sentimental. Without the peacemaking eagle the back Chapungu's warrior aspect would be simple brutality.

Whenever I see the photograph of Martin Luther King shaking Malcolm X's hand I think of the Chapungu.

As a peacemaker, Chapungu's work is involved with reweaving a world that has been torn asunder by violence: the courage of the warrior stepping forth now in the rites of heartbreak, confession, forgiveness and reconciliation.

When it comes to ngozi, Bantu medicine displays its true genius for it is here that one sees that the healing of the soul requires the healing of the community and the healing of the community requires the healing of the soul.

"I have witnessed this with my mother's brother," Mandaza tells me.

> He took a wife in a village, but he didn't know that a murder had happened there and an ngozi was tormenting his new woman. They had children together, but for years all she could say is "I want to go and kill myself."
>
> So finally my uncle went to his wife's relatives. They knew about this ngozi very well for they had done an evil thing. They told the ngozi, "This is your wife now. We have paid by giving this woman to you." The agreement with the spirit was that she was not supposed to be married at all!
>
> Finally she killed herself, and her ngozi started haunting their children. So far there are only two children left out of five. They were all dying.
>
> Now when they came to me, I told them to go and make peace with this ngozi because he needs rest. My uncle's wife was betrayed by her own family when they married her to this ngozi, but no one ever made peace with the ngozi and his kin. My spirits told me that the ngozi wants five head of cattle. "Bring them to his family," I said, "and there will be peace." They are in the process of doing that right now.

Someone who has spilt blood knows well the fury of ngozi, but it is the family of the slain that knows the spirits' grief. Healing ngozi, being freed of ngozi requires that one makes an alliance with grief. The lie that there is any other way is the lie that binds the soul to an enraged spirit, to a spirit of rage.

"If somebody comes to me with a ngozi," says Mandaza,

first I need to hear the story. The truth must come out of what
he did. We see if we cannot go to the family and talk to them
so that we are at peace. We cannot do any rituals until he con-
fesses. Then you do a ritual to send the ngozi away and initiate
the one who has confessed. But confession comes first.

The ngozi is not necessarily someone he has killed. It could
have been his brother or uncle or cousin. The reason it is following this particular man here is because he has some powerful
spirits, warriors but peacemakers as well who are saying, "Look
at what was done in our family." These spirits give him these
very powerful dreams so he sees the situation completely.

If someone came to me here whose brother had killed someone, I'd have him bring one or two of his family members, and
we talk about it. I ask my spirits what should be done, and then
I do it, and they are free. He can confess on his brother's behalf.
He apologizes to the spirit his brother has killed. He says, "I accept the evil of what he did. Let us make peace." And then I do
an initiation ceremony for him.

The two families must be brought together. Often one of the
members of the angered family will say, "Let us talk now. We
can't let things go on like this." In African culture if they want
five head of cattle, we take the cattle to them. They offer the
cattle to their ancestors, and they feast, and then there is peace.
Then we can cleanse this brother of the spirits that have tormented him and his family.

But if the other family refuses this peacemaking, we can
still do something about it. We talk directly to the spirits of
the people who are refusing, and we are given a dream about
what to do.

The townships here are filled with violence. They are filled
with ngozi, and they are driving families crazy. This is true
throughout the world.

Nightmares about soul-eating and avenging spirits paint a bleak picture of a community being attacked from both the outside and the inside, but there is no evidence that any of this is the bottom line for black America. No one is ever reducible to the forces that afflict them, but before Spirit can be called forth, we must look at the full implications of the hell that racism has created.

7

THE FATHER OF LIES

It was 6:00 a.m. and my shift was winding down: a few more pills to give and a simple dressing change.

Tyrone had slept well, an hourly dose of morphine automatically administered by a pump. I'd asked the nurses' aide to let him rest. Why wake him up at 4:00 for vital signs? Physically, at least, he was quite stable.

How do you approach the bed of a young man, Tyrone merely eighteen, who caught a bullet in the spine? The shock of waking up to the strange white nurse, smiling, awkward, trying to be respectful: "It's time for your morning dressing change."

"Oh, shit," groggy, remembering that he will never walk again. Shit. It's been only three days. The hole is more delicate than I would have expected, my little finger far too big to slide in. I remove saline gauze silently and use a q-tip to repack the wound with clean gauze. I rely on the tenderness of my fingers to distract myself from what cannot possibly be said, what in fact there are no words for.

Oh, shit. Shit. Shit. And more shit. The third young black man in two weeks with bullet wounds, one like Tyrone, paralyzed; another a college student visiting home for the holidays fortunate enough to have only his face blown away. Three. Only three, the homicide rate among black Americans being seven times that of whites. If I worked a few miles to the south at King-Drew Hospital, I might well appreciate what a small number three is.

In the early nineties, an anti-violence initiative was up for vote in Congress. Funding was sought so that blood could be drawn from children in the inner city — five, six, seven year olds — to test for genetic predisposition to violence. Those who tested positive could then be controlled with medications.

It is already considered legitimate medical practice to drug the children who we have and are systematically driving to the edge. Tens of millions of American children — black, white and other — are currently being drugged. This is regarded as an act of kindness, a skilled medical response to human anguish. Why not extend this kindness into social policy and drug black children "at risk"? How lucky for them, those at risk, that science can now identify and drug them, and how lucky for the communities they live in. It makes sense, doesn't it? After all, think of the money taxpayers will save on police, on building new prisons and maintaining the prisoners.

Kindness. Professionalism. Good fiscal sense.

Shit.

There are so many ways to eat the soul of another human being. So many ways and so many lies to convince oneself that one is acting respectably, responsibly, maybe even nobly. Dear God, what does it take to cut through the lie of respectability that would sacrifice another generation of black children with the same efficiency with which it is sacrificing young black men?

City planning, the birth of the slum, another effort (and in Africa it was often a "medical" effort) to keep white people safe from black disease, from the disease of blackness. In apartheid South Africa when plague was found in Cape Town and Johannesburg, the black townships were razed to the ground and the populace moved to sewage farms on the edge of the cities.

When blackness itself is regarded as a principle of disorder in an otherwise orderly white world, be it the black plague or violent crime, Bantu medicine has to ask the hard questions about how the individual and the community can transform the disease of white supremacy and those other diseases, all too human, that are aggravated by racism. The dark and nasty heart of racism allows whites a deluded sense of innocence and leaves some blacks with a sense that perhaps they were born into the realm of the damned and perhaps they will never escape. That in itself defines the boundaries of a diseased world.

Of course the narrowness of this world without air is reinforced by the layers of self-deception one wraps oneself in to survive an intolerable situation. One way "out" of the realm of the damned, after all, is to fold oneself into whiteness. "There but for the grace of God go I," declared Clarence Thomas as he spoke of his past as a poor black southerner before he became a darling of the Republican party. That is one tactic: the free man of color whose chain is so much longer than that of his brothers. bell hooks writes of the cost of that strategy:

> I am wiping the dust off past conversations to remember some of what was shared in the old days when black folks had little intimate contact with whites, when we were much more open about the way we connected whiteness with the mysterious, the strange, and the terrible. Of course, everything has changed. Now many black people live in the "bush of ghosts" and do not know themselves separated from whiteness. They do not know this thing we call "difference" . . . Yet blacks who imitate whites (adopting their values, speech, habits of being, etc.) continue to regard whiteness with suspicion, fear and even hatred. This contradictory longing to possess the reality of the Other, even though that reality is one that wounds and negates, is expressive of the desire to understand the mystery, to know intimately through imitation, as though such knowing worn like an amulet, a mask, will ward away the evil, the terror."

Imitating whites, one strategy for protecting oneself from spiritual cannibalism, is yet another way of serving up the soul to be eaten.

In some traditions such as European alchemy or Vajrayana Buddhism, one submits to the hard work of changing shit into gold or poison into nectar. We all know people who have suffered profoundly and have made beauty of it. In the African and the African-American world, these are the elders. In Bantu culture this work of transformation involves going into the darkness of suffering, confinement, circumstance and emerging initiated. I've largely avoided the "sociological" aspect of this domain of confinement — the stuff of everyday news - but "everybody knows" that the camarinha exists on every level of society and relationship, chaining spirit and soul within the house of bondage.

In the past three chapters, Mandaza and I have looked at dreams of spiritual slavery, soul-eating (muti), and avenging spirits (ngozi). Spiritual slavery and muti/ngozi form a single complex internally reinforced by its own self-defining patterns on both the level of society and the individual. Lived out according to its logic, this complex will and does draw blacks both in the Motherland and in the diaspora to kill each other and eat each other's souls. The circumstances are arranged so that what white supremacy cannot do directly, it leaves in the hands of blacks.

The soul is put in a bottle. Call it the inner city, a township, a prison, a school, a job; call it America or just say that you feel all bottled up inside, that something's eating you. And in that bottle is placed a few ngozi. Your child has nightmares. Your teenage boy is looking dangerous. A lot of anger in the household or the neighborhood. The witchcraft that is the nature of everyday life makes you powerless against the dead that cry out for justice. The laments of the restless dead leave you defenseless against a soul-eating system.

The Greeks have a word for such a situation: aporia, the illusion of no exit, no escape. Lewis Hyde uses the example of the humpback whale who, when it comes upon a school of herring,

> dives deep and then swims in a slow circle, exhaling all the while so that a cone of bubbles rises through the water. The herring in the school misperceive this "bubble net" as a barrier through which they cannot swim. Having confined the school, the whale then rises through the center of the bubble net, its mouth open and filling with fish.

"To experience aporia," writes Hyde,

> is to be caught in a tunnel with a fire at either end, to be be-
> wildered by clouds of ink or encircled by a net of bubbles. No
> matter how many times you reverse yourself, you're still caught.
> Aporia is the trap of bafflement, invented by a being whose
> hunger has made him or her more cunning than those who only
> think to travel forward through a transparent world.

Every African American knows the experience of aporia intimately: hooks's "bush of ghosts," damned if you do and damned
if you don't, the camarinha where the slave/initiate learns the
meaning of what it is to be unfree, the rememories where the
ancestors cry out for emancipation.

An "octopus darkens the water with a jet of ink," Hyde
continues,

> turning transparency into a murky, impenetrable, nonporous
> medium . . . [As with the humpback whale,] the impenetrability
> is an illusion. The darkness around the octopus is only an arti-
> ficial night; the herring are trapped not by bubbles but by their
> own defenses and perceptive limitations. Still, in each case the
> artifice suffices.

I try not to exaggerate or trivialize this moment of anguish.
Some will see what I mean, and others will dismiss it, but Hyde
provides an essential insight: "Artifice suffices." The devil that is
white supremacy, not white people, is the father of lies; and the
truth will, in fact, set you free.

There are various paths that lead to the moment of yielding
to truth, to initiation, so that Spirit can enter an afflicted world,
but there is, also, only one path, only one prayer. At the bottom
of initiation, in Africa as in America, you are halfway across the
River Jordan, and a current begins to pull you under. If you try
to rescue yourself, you will surely drown. It may have worked
in the past, but this is different. Your life is at stake and if not
your life, your soul. You cry out to Spirit because everything in
you wants to live. For once you forget that you feel unworthy of

life, forget that you don't even know what the word freedom means; something profound and unnameable rises up to cry out for life, for freedom, and you yield to the prayer. And Spirit comes. Always surprising, always inevitable. Spirit comes and brings you to the other shore. You know that you will never be the same and that your spirits will remain free as long as you serve the Spirit of freedom in yourself and others. The questions on which you had based your life begin to change — not now how do I break free from spiritual slavery but how do I make my life hospitable to Spirit, a vehicle for Spirit's desire to heal? And again, how do I sing the Lord's song in a strange land?

8

TO GO THROUGH

Ghosts, dogs and water
Crossing Jordan
Fear guarding the edges of the camarinha, defining the edge of
the world in which one is enslaved. Aporia. No way out
To go through. Fear. To go through fear. The fear of going
through. The fear that carries one through to the other side.
Fear of ghosts, dogs and water.

Words reveal their deepest meanings when they are followed to their origins. If you dig into the underground Indo-European stream of meanings, fear, for example, comes from the Sanskrit "to go through." It is actually related to the word "ferry," as Webster says, "to take across a river or narrow body of water in a boat." It is also related to the word "fare," the amount of money paid for transportation. In ancient Greek myth one paid the ferryman Charon to take one over to the realm of the dead. So also among the Lodagaa of West Africa, the fare being twenty cowries.

Tsehai Farrell says,

> African-Americans in group consciousness, not necessarily as individuals, have three primary fears that we just took for granted from the time we were little kids: ghosts, dogs and water.

Tsehai's statement surprised me for two reasons. Firstly, I had never heard it said before or at least not so simply and completely. I'd noticed the fear many black Americans have of

dogs, and I've had many conversations about ghosts and demons, but to hear these three fears stated in a single sentence
was startling because in Central Africa "ghosts, dogs and water"
belong to the passage to the realm of the ancestors undertaken
in initiation. To be paralyzed by these three fears is to be cut
off from that world.

In this chapter I'd like to braid together Tsehai's, Mandaza's and
my own insights regarding ghosts, dogs and water, but first I must
warn against literalism, that very American disease that makes it
impossible to understand fear, much less go through it.

In the spirit world when we talk about ghosts, dogs and water, it should be clear that we're not necessarily speaking of literal ghosts, four-legged mammals, and H_2O. We are talking about
the spirits that rise up and frighten us when we undertake the
passage between worlds. One can always numb oneself to literal
fears or deny them or do some manner of behavioral modifica-
tion, but this deprives fear of the possibility of transforming us if
we move with and through it. Ghosts, dogs and water speak of a
specific terrain of fear and transformation. Although initiation is
never a simple act of passing from one "stage" to another, I think
the traditional Bantu way of understanding this geography offers
a useful mirror, and I will write of it "as if" one passes over in
stages. In other words, there is a geography to initiation, but there
will never be a map. Nonetheless, I will write as if there is.

"Oh, yes," says Mandaza, "My people are also afraid of these
things. So much so."

It has been Mandaza's and my experience that it is virtually
impossible to initiate someone who refuses to feel fear. In the
ngoma of the water spirits, fear stands close to both awe and
humility. "Twas grace that taught my heart to fear, and grace my
fear relieved." Awe, humility — and gratitude.

After talking to Tsehai, I informally posed the question to a
number of black friends and acquaintances about ghosts, dogs
and water. By and large Tsehai's insight was confirmed: One,
two or three out of three fears rang true. The exception was
a rather brittle and macho fellow who seemed to think I was

casting aspersions on his manhood by suggesting he was afraid of anything at all.

Much has already been said of ghosts — spooks, ngozi — those spirits who look so much like white people. Tsehai's comments are worth adding.

> For black people whites have no substance. They are ghostlike. A lot of black people think white people can't even move, can't walk, have no grace to them. They don't have whatever attaches you to core kinds of things. They are detached from something. I've watched children ask "Who are they?" It's a question that can't be talked about because we're trapped by a culture which is dangerous and they own it. You can't say bad things about the jailers. A lot of black people think whites are scary in an essential kind of way because they are not grounded in life; to be more accurate, that they are another kind of life form. It really goes that far. Because they have so much power, we have to pretend like we're comfortable, but we're afraid of them because they don't seem to answer to the same God.

One of the Kikongo words for the realm of the ancestors is ku mfinda, literally "in the forest." After actual death or after the spiritual death through which one must pass in order to be reconciled with Spirit, it is felt that one moves beyond the edge of the village and into and through the bush. The village is encircled by warrior spirits who protect the living from the dangers of the wild. Outside the village, as Devisch explained, are the spirits of foreigners (aka whites), monstrous spirits, predatory animals, evil sorcerers, and the revengeful deceased (ngozi). Speaking broadly, it is here, just beyond the realm of the known world that one has to face the ghosts.

Mandaza speaks of the diplomatic relationship the nganga has with these spirits:

> In our own African culture, when we do a ritual, we brew a pot of beer and roast some meat to take outside the village and feed those spirits in the bush. When they are feasting, we do our rituals at home, and they don't interfere. This way we separate the spirits of the bush from the spirits of the village.

For Bantu people this diplomacy stands alongside the fierce integrity of the warrior spirits and the nganga's alliance with the warriors. This was reflected in the spiritual I quoted in Chapter 2:

> We'll cross de might Myo
> My army cross over
> O. Pharaoh's army drowned!
> My army cross over.

Mandaza explains,

> After you die, you have to fight off ghosts on the way to the an-cestors. The ghosts want to prevent you from going to the good ancestors. They want to capture you on the way, but there are so many warriors around you, you go straight to the good ancestors. After you are initiated, those good ancestors will make use of you to help their people who are living on this earth.

Mandaza gives an example of Pamba, a young Shona man he initiated.

> When I met him, he was almost mentally disturbed. He had no protection at all. He came to me with a very strong dream. He would see a skeleton of a human being in front of him, and when it would get close, Pamba would get out of his senses. At other times he would see a big flame of fire in front of him, and he would get frightened. My warrior spirits would come and chase away these terrible visions, and I'd use water and the sweat lodge and herbs for smoking to call his warrior spirits to come to protect him and to give him the courage to look fear in the eye.

Ghosts carry the image of whatever we are afraid of: phan-toms, the phantasms of our fears, skeletons, walls of flame, white people. This is a moment of radical authenticity where, as Mandaza says, fear must be looked in the eye. To lie is to make oneself the food of ghosts. This is also where one pays one's fare of twenty cowrie shells to Spirit as a token of recognizing one's complete dependence. Without Spirit, one will never make it through the land of ghosts.

Beyond the land of ghosts, the Bantu say, there is a village of dogs.

"My people are also afraid of dogs," says Mandaza,

> especially when the dogs appear in the form of warriors who are trying to protect them. When the dogs try to fight the ghosts that are on the people, they think the dogs are haunted. The dogs bark at evil spirits, but people think they are barking at them, and that situation creates fear in them. But it is the fear that is dividing people from their ancestors!
>
> Take Pamba, for example. When I started initiating him, he was so afraid of dogs. So afraid! And for a while it seemed that his fear was getting worse until I finally told him, "Don't you understand that we ngangas are the dogs of God! Why do you think I'm always chasing away ghosts? Why do you think I am always finding the path for you?" When he understood that I was God's dog, he laughed and began to calm down. He laughed, but not everybody does. Some people are afraid of ngangas and dogs because we have four eyes and can see invisible things.
>
> If a dog comes in your dreams and it bites you, then there must be an evil spirit following after you, and the dog is trying to chase it away to protect you. Dogs are especially sensitive to evil spirits because they have a hunter spirit in them. They can smell spirits and identify them. Once you make friends with the dog, you can pass through to the village of the ancestors with much more confidence.

In passing through the land of ghosts, one is moving through the thicket of one's own fears. It is a time of self- recognition, self-confrontation, persistence and faith — faith even when one feels most lost. Things shift, however, when one comes into the village of dogs. Should one feel afraid of dogs, this is the moment one is required to befriend fear, to make an ally of it for without dog spirit one will never find one's way to the village of the ancestors. Dog is faithful. Dog knows how to follow its nose. Dog can find the path from the village to the land of the dead and back again.

In the Kongo, writes Wyatt MacGaffey, "the most important animal is the dog, which lives with man and has no counterpart in the forest. Dogs are said to have blood like a man's; being also animals, they can see the dead." Some mojo that are used to keep close to the path are addressed as dogs:

"But aren't you a dog with four eyes?"

As far as I know, it was Theodore P. Ford who first connected African-Americans fear of dogs with the Egyptian God Anubis, which is to say we are speaking of a stratum of Bantu/African-American culture that is more than 3,000 years old. In 1939 Ford wrote:

> The dog, which is universally regarded as man's best friend, among the American blacks is more than just a friend; he is a creature endowed with supernatural prowess. It is the spirit of the dog which warns one of the approach of death . . . Students of Negro and Egyptian folklore will readily see in this superstition elements common to the Egyptian belief in the Dog-God Anubis. The Egyptian Dog-God's duty was to escort the soul through the realms of the dead.

For many people who have left behind their old life and are trying to find the path back to their origins, dog spirit appears simply with that sudden alertness to the "signs." Things are not what they used to be. Strange coincidences seem to be happening; a stranger may say something to you that penetrates to the heart of things; the exactly "right" book that you need to read now drops into your lap; you are dreaming more than usual; you follow intuitions when in the past you were inclined to be more "reasonable"; chance events suddenly take on significance, and you try to read them. This is dog spirit following its nose, leading you onward through an invisible landscape. Dog is teaching you to see through another set of eyes.

Having left behind the village of ghosts or in coming to new thresholds where yet more ghosts live, dog spirit is an invaluable companion. Quite often, however, it is darkest before the dawn. In THE EGYPTIAN BOOK OF THE DEAD, the bleakest hour of the night journey is called Unu-T4-5, and it feels as if the soul itself is about to be snuffed out. Sometimes this is experienced as a field of ash: meaninglessness, the signs one had relied upon now completely absent. Sometimes there are too many signs, and one is engulfed by them and led hither and thither. Sometimes even dog departs, or so it seems, and one is left with the intimacy of prayer and the shedding of tears. Whatever happens between the village and the domain of the ancestors must be folded back into sacred understanding. "The road we walk is very hard," sings Mandaza's wife Simakuhle, "therefore kneel down and pray."

Regarding the fear of water, Tsehai says,

> So many African-Americans are afraid of water. We used to say we didn't go into the water because you pressed your wet hair and it'll get all nappy, but boys didn't go into the water either. Maybe it was the trans-Atlantic slave trade, so many millions underneath the sea. Growing up, if I met a black person who knew how to swim, it was very unusual. It is only now it seems more are swimming.

This passage through initiatory death, through the geography of fear and through the village of dogs is ultimately, God willing, a journey to the village of the water spirits. Remember the West African priest of the water spirits that Gleason interviewed said that he knew that his tradition was safe because "contact with water by its very nature safeguards the primordial secrets." To submit to water, to be immersed and to reemerge is to die in God and be reborn. When one is well prepared, this baptismal moment is one of holy fear, necessity, delight and even ecstasy. As Mandaza says of Pamba,

> I used the powers given to me by my spirits to remove the obstacles, and he saw the ancestors coming out of the water and saying, "We are coming closer to you now."

I was once discussing the way of the water spirits with my friend Peter Leavitt. Peter is shuso, or head monk at a Zen Buddhist monastery in Northern California. He said he understood me well, that his spiritual practice completely changed when he realized that those called "Buddha ancestors," he said, "have worked for my liberation and the liberation of all beings since before I was born." To submit to the water spirits is to step unchained from the camarinha, out of the narrow aporia of white supremacy and into the light of God.

As with ghosts and dogs, the fear of water needn't be understood literally. When Malcolm X talks about the fear of surrendering to Allah, among Bantu people his fear might well be understood as water spirit illness. Going through the fear is the path itself. As the Bakongo Lemba song says, "That which was the sickness, has become the path to the priesthood."

The fear of ghosts, dogs and water is actually the stuff of everyday life, made vivid and intensified within initiation, to be sure, but it's always best not to exoticize the way of transformation.

One "goes through" fear so that someday one might yield to water. This yielding — initiation — is the true beginning of life in the Spirit and will be explored in depth in the next section. For most African Americans, initiation happens within everyday life, or it doesn't happen at all. Ghosts abound. Being real with one's fears, seeing through fear, is necessary if one is to go beyond a narrow existence. "Dog spirits," those faithful friends and teachers who come to one's aid when one is spiritually lost, are out there if one looks for them. And the moment will come when one has to choose whether or not to take the plunge and go beneath the surface of this life.

I have come to the water

      for great things happened
      on the day I was born
      when they sat my mother down
      by the pool of blood

      For this reason I have come,
      have returned as a child

      Mu kinkenda kia bana bame
      out of compassion for my children

              Kingani
              Matadi (Zaire), 1971

THE VILLAGE
OF THE ANCESTORS,
THE LIVING AND THE UNBORN

9

MAY THE CIRCLE BE UNBROKEN

One afternoon while I was being initiated, Mandaza gathered the clan together around a ceramic pot containing water made thick and murky with white clay. "Eat as much of this as you can," he said, "but remember this is not food for you; it is food for the ancestors."

While I was writing the first chapter of this book, I had a chance conversation with my friend Sarah MacEnany. Sarah grew up in Pike County, Georgia. I was somewhat lost in researching the Bantu presence in Georgia and areas thereabout; so I asked her if she knew anything about the ways of the local black folk. She confessed that the racial divide was such that she really didn't except that black Georgians seemed to have a fondness for eating white clay. Apparently white clay is sold in the Circle-K convenience stores, and behind her house there was a clay pit that was used by the locals. When I encouraged her to talk to her mother about this, her mother claimed she didn't know why they ate white clay, that it was "just a custom."

Sarah then gave me the phone number of Annette Patterson, an African-American friend who lives in Florida. Annette recalled driving south of Virginia with a black friend and pulling over when she spied some white clay at the roadside. "I got to get some for my aunt," she explained. Her Virginian friend was puzzled. "African Americans don't eat clay where he came from," she told me, "but in the Carolinas and Georgia, it's pretty common." The Carolinas and Georgia were the American colonies/states most overwhelmingly influenced by Central African culture.

In Chapter One I spoke of mpemba, the Bantu word for white clay and the realm of the ancestors. John Janzen writes of the ceremonial color term "pemba, white clay or river chalk, denotative of 'clarity' or 'purity,' [that it is] an attribute of the ancestors." Eating white clay, having it smeared over the surface of the body or merely ringing the eyes is common in rites of initiation. "Whiteness," writes Janzen, "defines the status of the novice, who, from the time of initial entry until graduation, is 'in the white.'"

Over the past few years it had been the source of great consternation to me that roughly a third of the dreams I've collected from African Americans have images of benevolent, mysterious and sometimes supernaturally powerful whites. I simply did not know what to do with these dreams. One reading would be that white supremacy had infected the black psyche with idealized images of whiteness. Dr. Na'im Akbar has written eloquently in Chains and Images of Psychological Slavery of the effect of blacks being surrounded by images of white angels, the white Christ and his Heavenly Father, also undoubtedly white. Akbar has written quite sensibly that God must not be colorized.

It apparently required that I be initiated in and through 'the white' before I was able to drop the obtusely American habit of racializing these dreams. In Zimbabwe these dreams are manifestly not about white people; they are about water spirits that very often (though not always) appear white in the dreams of Africans.

A couple of weeks after my first initiation, I dreamt that I was walking along a mud road through the Zambezi rain forest. Approaching from a distance, I saw a "white man" wearing old work clothes. Uncommonly white, almost translucent. There was an uncanny grace to him. He paused before a tree and clapped his hands quietly in the traditional Shona gesture that asks permission of the forest before one picks herbs and climbed the tree swiftly to perhaps thirty feet. He ate leaves from a clinging vine without touching them and then climbed down. I took out my snuff container and tapped bute into my hand, sniffed a little and blessed the road with the remainder. Although we didn't interact, I recognized this man as a water spirit, a spirit nganga, an ally. We did not even meet each others' eyes, and yet the subtlest mutual acknowledgment was there as we passed each other on the road. The following morning I asked Mandaza why it is that water spirits often appear as white people.

"They are clean spirits," Mandaza replied. "If there is dark in them, initiation has to be done to make them clean."
"Does that mean," I asked, "that when spirits come in the form of black people, they are unclean spirits?"

> Oh, no. The element of torment must be there. They must be violent or troublesome. None of this has to do with race. We offer a white sheep that there be peace and love and unity in the world. Whenever you are at war and you want peace, you raise the white flag. White means peace, justice, the truth, submission to higher authority."

It was the dreams of Jonathan Morris who first alerted me to the presence of water spirits in the soul of black Americans:

> I looked at this water turn to people, mostly black kids and white people with big stomachs and loud voices that sounded like a drum.

When I read this dream to Mandaza, he laughed with delight for he knows well how the drum draws water spirits into the bodies of the community.

> This spirit is for all people. Water is a spirit for people of all colors. This man has water spirits that appear in the form of black and white people. The loud cries and the big stomachs mean they are rejoicing. They are well fed! In ngoma the voice of the spirit is in drumming. When his initiation is done, this particular person must have music.

Mr. Morris also dreamt:

> I was in a tent in the desert with all these white women, and
> they had hair as black as night, and they treated me like a king.
> I wanted water, but they wouldn't give it to me. I stood up, and
> they started to fade away and become invisible. Soon I was
> standing alone in a river.

"See how it is," says Mandaza,

> that the njuzu come out of water like this and disappear into
> water? That's the way it is in my dreams too. That is why I some-
> times call them mermaids.
>
> This dream has nothing to do with oppression of men by
> men. It is a message to the dreamer. His spirits were waiting for
> him. He needs to be initiated in water. He hadn't been initiated;
> so the mermaids wouldn't give him water. To be among the wa-
> ter spirits and be deprived of water is one kind of water spirit
> disease. He must be immersed in water and reunited with his
> spirits. There is an invisible obstacle in this dream that prevents
> him from receiving anything from his spirits.
>
> The njuzu can come in any form, but the long hair is one way
> we identify them from ordinary people. Sometimes it is a black
> person with long hair; that is why my spirits have told me to
> braid my hair the way I do. It is like the flowing of the water. Or
> it is like Grandmother Spider with her long legs; the hair con-
> nects the spirit to the surrounding area.

William Dubois, a janitor and co-worker at the hospital offered me a similar dream:

> I was with a group of white ladies, and it was like in Roman
> times, and they were giving me a bath in what looked like a
> pool, but there wasn't any water in it. I felt like I was lost.

Mandaza comments,

> His spirits are abandoning him; he reaches out to them, and they
> disappear. How can you bathe without water? That is why he
> feels lost. He needs very strong initiation.

In the first initiation he'll be able to touch his spirits, no question. I would remove whatever obstacles, and his spirits would gather around him and be close to him.

Some dreams especially emphasize the non-human nature of the spirits. James Draper, in his late forties, by profession a stockbroker, dreamt,

I was on the edge of a cliff, and a spaceship approached me from behind, and I don't know if you want to call these white people or what, but they were white like milk. They wanted to help me to a place I was looking for on the other side of this big lake; so they put me into this thing that looked like a giant bug, and we rode off. We came to a dam, and I looked behind me, and all these milk-colored people were skating on the water. That's how they traveled.

Gliding over water or flying. Mxolisi, a Zulu woman from South Africa dreamt,

I see a white woman who demonstrated how she is able to fly very high and drop from her flight into an open window. I look at her and admire her ability, and then I'm reminded that I too am able to be that agile with my body, but I do it in a different way. So I articulate this to her, saying, "My ability is different in that I fly closer to the ground . . ." And I am satisfied that this level gets me to where I need to be.

Mandaza disagrees with the assessment of this woman's dream spirit. "The spirits are with her," he says,

but she needs initiation, probably by the Zulu people. She must fly at the same height as her spirits. They must fly together. She thinks she's okay as she is, flying close to the ground. But that's not the case at all.

Wealth is a common theme in water spirit dreams. When one sees white spirits in situations of wealth, it's tempting to read the dream in terms of class politics — white folks have more resources — rather than in terms of a parallel spiritual world of fertility and generosity. But long before colonialism imposed a cash economy and a racial caste system, it was understood that the water spirits governed rainfall, the fertility and the generosity of the earth as well as the material beneficence of the king and queen. One sees a remnant of this in contemporary Botswana where the local currency is called "pula" — rain. Placing a dream of Teresa's (my patient with sickle cell anemia that I mentioned in Chapter 2) alongside one of Mxolisi's gives a feel for this realm of water spirit imagery in two black women, one American, the other African.

Teresa dreamt:

> There was this farm with an old shack attached to a mansion. The farm was divided in half: white trash (they were poor but nice) on one side and rich white people on the other. On the side of the poor folks, there were cows and pigs, but on the rich side it was like Rodeo Drive and Sak's Fifth Avenue.
>
> I have a twin sister, but she's white even though we have the same mother. She's real poor, a kind of Ellie Clampett type. You know the Beverly Hillbillies? We dress alike and can even fool people even though I'm blue black and she's snow white. Sometimes we date the same boyfriend, and he doesn't even notice.
>
> She has a baby that's striped red and green. My baby is striped black and white.
>
> The grass on the rich people's side is super green, but it's not really grass: it's like a pool of water, and there are fish swimming in it. The rich people can walk on water.
>
> The sky isn't blue: it's fluorescent pink. It glows in the dark on the rich people's side, but it doesn't shine at all on the poor people's side.
>
> The horses live at the boundary with their bodies half on one side, half on the other. On the rich people's side, they are beautiful thoroughbreds, but the parts of their bodies on the poor people's side are like old swaybacked work horses. When they turn around, it's just the same; their bodies change, depending on which part is on what side of the line.

It's the same with me if I stand at the boundary. On one side I'm wearing a diamond tennis bracelet, and on the other it's just a ring of dirty, rusty nails. On one side it's a mink coat, and on the other it's overalls.

My twin and I have to choose sides; so I go for the rich side of the farm, but after I do, the sides shift, and I'm poor again.

The reader may recall that Teresa is a twin in her waking life. This has to be taken into account when her dream soul recognizes a twin white sister. Twins are universally regarded as children of the water spirits in parts of Bantu Africa and by their nature have a foot in this world and the parallel world of the ancestors. In Teresa's dream, the other world, the world of the water spirits, is one she is both exiled from and is in intimate relationship with. It is the miraculous beneficence of water that transforms the dry earth to grass which is greener then green, the broken horse to a thoroughbred, the rusty nails to a diamond bracelet.

This one still wants to take on the culture of white people, to go the way of darkness. Once she is initiated, it will be easy for her to cross back and forth from this world to the village of the water spirits.

Mxolisi's dream also touches on the relation between fertility, money and the water spirits.

I am aware of being in a drama, in some kind of play, and the main players or actors are white. I get the feeling that I am facilitating this drama in some way. It is a drama about life, and it is happening on my right side. Then there comes a "church scene," and it seems again that this church is all white, and they are singing a hymn that is familiar to me and my culture . . . The minister then comes towards me and hands me an offering from him and his congregation. I do not understand why he is offering this to me, and I wonder if I should accept it, but I do, along with its mystery . . . I am on a path, and I throw the money down on the path in front of me . . . Suddenly the road becomes like a river rushing with water, taking the money along with it.

If I go after the money, I will be washed away with it. I decide
to let the water and the money struggle with themselves, and I
begin to walk across some beautiful African fields. It seems like
mid spring. I return to my family.

Mandaza's understanding of this dream:

Ah! She returns to her family. The spirit is saying no matter how
much money you make, go back to your ancestors. They will
give you riches from water. Throwing the money down means
she must give up the world she is living in for the water spirits
because they are the ones that make the fields green."

I once listed the qualities of water spirit dreams featuring
"whites" that I've found common among Bantu and African-
American people:

An association with water, blueness, greenness,
fertility and by extension wealth and good luck;
People walking on water;
Healing miracles;
Generosity and tranquility, a sense of an ordered world;
An association with fish;
Telepathy or a secret language;
Ritual activity, usually in circles;
Message bearers, "angels," beings of light;
Associations of purity and cleanliness;
An erotic nymphlike quality, "pure" eros;
Protection;
Appearing and disappearing in thin air;
Airiness, whites flying or defying gravity;
Association with clouds, elusiveness, shapeshifting.

To generalize broadly, blacks in these dreams seem to be of
the earth and earthiness; whites are creatures of water and air.

This domain is called the village of the water spirits. It is
mysterious beyond telling, difficult to get to and yet no further
than a generous and kind heart, a sense of purpose in life, and
the lived knowledge of God's benevolence. In previous chapters

I've explored how white supremacy throws up every conceivable obstacle to block the efforts of the soul to be reunited with Spirit; I have seen how racism fractures the field of relationship where Spirit wants to move; I have looked at spiritual slavery, as real now, Mandaza says, as when blacks were bought and sold. When we yield to water, we yield to these spirits who are unfettered by time and history and are therefore capable of setting the soul free and reminding it why it chose to be born, to even be born black and American.

The circle was imported from the Kongo to the American South. The water spirits seem to like to gather in circles, little eddies into which are drawn everything that one needs to know so that it all can be given over freely and generously. Tommy Walters, the homeless man who (Mandaza thought) mistook a white witch doctor for a water spirit, gave me this dream:

> I was in the midst of a group of men of all races. We were gathered in a circle with five torches surrounding us, casting our shadows on white walls. We were dressed in cream-colored hooded robes, talking telepathically to one another and waiting for God. We could not wear our shoes or sandals. There was a pool created in the beginning of the world, and we had to bathe in it before we could enter the ivory-colored chamber.
>
> We knew how we had each lived on earth and that we had died or at least went through great problems in our different countries. We also had a mission which we didn't finish, but maybe this was what we all had in common. Yet in the midst of us, suspended in the air, was a huge scroll in a language we could all understand.
>
> After looking at the scroll, the walls began to open up with cylinders where we laid back into a white cottonlike fabric, one at a time, each with a scroll in our hands. A great mist came out of the chamber, and we all disappeared. After this dream, I often wonder — is this a calling or a gathering?

10

EVEN AS I AM KNOWN

The Yoruba tell a wonderful story about Yemaya, the mother of the gods, who is also the ocean, and her son Shango, the spirit of lightening and fire.

It seems that Shango had become a man about town, bar hopping, boasting of his sexual prowess and looking for one-night stands.

When Yemaya heard rumors of this, she decided to put a stop to her son's shameful behavior. Disguising herself as the sort of woman Shango liked best, not so much innocent but juicy, she went to one of his favorite haunts and waited for him to make his evening rounds.

Yemaya watched her son enter the bar and scrutinize the women, deftly avoiding those he had been with before until he was struck by the beauty of this woman he did not know.

She pretended to ignore him for a while, but after Shango approached her with all his charm, she conceded to a dance.

Afterwards, sitting at a table, she invited him with an occasional glance, letting him touch her hand and ensured that he got more than a little drunk on rum. When the time was ripe, she said, "Why don't we go for a walk on the beach?"

Shango was inflamed. He could taste his triumph.
And so they strolled on the beach under a full moon. Shango looked away from the shore for a cluster of trees or a fisherman's shack, a private place where he might take this gor-

geous woman. When Yemaya suggested that they climb into her boat, a small barely enclosed little dinghy tied to a tiny pier, Shango agreed.

Now, among those who walk on land, Shango's machismo was legendary, but there was one thing that truly terrified him, and that was to be out at sea. He felt a bit nervous about the little boat, but when he looked at Yemaya under the moonlight, his desire was almost more than he could bear.

After a few caresses and an attempted kiss, Shango was lost. He didn't even notice when Yemaya quietly untied the boat.

Shango was so consumed by his yearning and the anticipation of his conquest that they were rather far out at sea before he looked up and realized it.

He began trembling and stuttering. "You witch," he cried out, "why did you bring me here? What are you going to do to me?"

When Yemaya saw that he was completely broken and helpless, she dipped her hand in the sea water, washed off her makeup and let her hair down. Then Shango realized that he had attempted to seduce his own mother.

"I did not raise my son to dishonor women," she said. "Have you no shame? Get up and row us to the shore like a man and change your ways."

Shango did what he was told. At the shore he turned his back to his mother and walked away, but he was never the same again.

When it comes to sex and spirituality, what are the stories we were born into? And what implications do these stories have in our intimate lives?

Very few religious traditions, short of Greek Orthodox monasticism, split sexuality from spirituality as thoroughly as the Protestantism that has influenced black and white American culture. In a broad mythological way, one could say Yemaya is the African equivalent of Mary, and Shango, being a dying and resurrected god, is like Jesus. But then it's difficult to imagine

Christ as a swaggering Lothario or the Blessed Virgin dressing hot and sexy in order to teach him a lesson. While pre-Christian European folk culture is rich with such lusty stories, the permissible stories that the Puritans transplanted in the American colonies are another thing altogether.

Splitting spirituality from sexuality tends to leave Americans stranded between puritanism and pornography with very little imaginative room to honor the sacred power of desire and to delight in it. This affects our lives on every level but most severely distorts the relationship between men and women.

Tsehai has encouraged me to write a little about the Bantu understanding of sacred sexuality, both the sacredness of the erotic embrace but also the erotic relationship between soul and Spirit. I am, frankly, shy, but I'll try not to let that distract me. For one thing, white supremacy and the puritanical tradition that sustains it has done enormous violence against black sexuality. Aside from the soul-eating myths that separate sex and spirit and an ugly history of the rape of black women, there is the white nightmare that black people are wrapped in: white paranoia of "black" sexuality coupled with a longing for "it." "It" is a hallucinatory fantasy of black sexuality, vitality and virility, longed for and punished.

I once went with my wife Deena to a small restaurant in Pasadena to watch an old blues singer do her thing. I confess I can't recall her name, but I do remember that she was in her seventies, quite drunk, damn talented, wary, amiable, and looking extraordinarily weary. Two white couples shared a table near us, and one of the men at that table asked repeatedly for her to sing "Put a Little Sugar in My Bowl." She shined him on, but he persisted, and she finally conceded.

Her rendition of this song was indescribable. She did it impeccably, but what was truly remarkable is how expertly she measured out venom, the edge of refusing to be humiliated by singing this song to a white man who had no clue. Her expertise was such that I saw no evidence whatsoever that the white man even noticed the bitter undertones she brought into the sexiest of songs though her contempt was aimed directly at him by way of indirection. He and his table applauded wildly. I was stunned. This woman, drunk as she was, knew how to defend herself against a witch.

In CAPABLE OF SUCH BEAUTY I write about "it" at great length for "it" is the linchpin that holds together the racist world view. Suffice it to say that in the context of this book, "it", white people's fantasies of black sexuality, is just another dream that ensnares black souls in order to eat them.

I once spent a couple of years pondering the Navajo emergence myth because I felt these people had something to teach me about what they call "walking in beauty." In the story the ancestors of the Navajo, the wind spirit creatures, the nilchii dine'e, migrated from world to world beneath this earth surface world. These insubstantial creatures were always getting into trouble sexually. Being taken in by different tribes, say in the first or the second or the third world, the little nilchii dine'e would end up having sex with the husbands or wives of the beings that gave them refuge. And so they would be kicked out. Over and again they made the same mistake and seemed incapable of learning from past experience. It was not until emerging through a hole in the ground somewhere in Southwest Colorado that the ancestors taught order to the wind spirit creatures, and they became human, "those with five fingers." The story is about sexuality being rendered intelligent, the emergence of an ordered world alongside an intelligently lived sexuality. In this earth surface world, one participates in beauty by making beauty. It is not as if beauty is itself sexualized but that one cannot see the beauty of this life or walk in balance without honoring the codes that protect the profundity of the sexual act.

The Bantu understanding of sexuality is far closer to the Navajo point of view than to a puritanism that can't begin to imagine sexual intelligence. Initiation, coming of age, being an adult and honoring the way of the ancestors are very tied up with the tenderness and intelligence that one brings to the erotic life.

The story of Yemaya and Shango can only be understood in the light of Shango's death and resurrection. It seems that when he was king, Shango had gotten carried away with "lightening medicine," the magic and power of calling forth the thunderstorm. The potency of this "medicine" went to his head, and he lost perspective. One day lightening struck the palace and burnt to death his wives and children. Out of his mind with grief over the irreversible damage his egotism had done, he ran off into the forest and hung himself by the neck.

The king is dead. Long live the king.

As in the story with Yemaya, the spirit of Shango is always involved in the tempering of the soul. The exuberant wielding of power, including here the fire of sexuality, is dangerous. The blade is perfected by returning it to the fire, flattening it between hammer and anvil, folding it over on itself, flattening it again, folding it until the steel is tempered. As Mandaza says, "The warrior's eye must be as sharp as his blade, or there will be trouble." This folding and flattening and refolding is the persistent work of self-reflection, especially after one has acted blindly, so that sexuality and power can be carried with grace. So many of the stories talk about the young Shango full of bluster and uncontained exuberance. We like these stories. All of us have met such young men. Few, however, speak of the old king, the warrior who bears the blade of justice, as profound a healer as there is among the spirits. How many see the final blade radiant, glorious in its exactitude — God coming forth as thunderbolt?

Among Bantu people, the Shango who was reprimanded by his mother was very much lost in what is called "red" sexuality. Red is the sexuality between the village and the bush, the car parked at the edge of town or at the drive-in theater. It is a given that teenagers are "in the red," quite uncontrollable. "In the red" characterizes worlds of sexual experimentation which is the proper domain of adolescents but in America sometimes reemerges after a divorce, for example, or in midlife. There is a play in being sexy, strutting it, knowing one's potency, exhilarating in the sheer power of desire. Delight and danger belong to red sexuality, delight of every sort — feeling one's oats and sowing them wildly. Danger is also quite real, ranging from sexual coercion, betrayal, unplanned pregnancy, to death. In Africa red sexuality has become outright lethal with the breakdown of the traditional rites of initiation, which open the long path of realigning desire with the way of the ancestors. This was made clear to me by a young HIV-positive patient of mine in Bulawayo whose sex life could only be described as homicidal, his own fear of death not at all dampening the pleasures of seduction.

Red sexuality is sexuality before tempering. It is unreflected upon. It is innocent even when it does damage because it is moving blindly according to its own urgencies and hasn't quite grasped that other people truly exist. I never sensed any evil intent in my "homicidal" patient, just a radical lack of self-reflection about the consequences of his actions. As with the young Shango, pleasure and willfulness often get confused, the willfulness of pleasure, the pleasure of unimpeded will.

For Western Bantu people initiation of teenage girls involved entering into erotic intelligence. The girl is separated from her daily work to live in semi-seclusion in an initiatory hut. Here she is well fed and taken care of by the older women. To be attractive, she is encouraged to fatten up since feminine beauty requires a little flesh on the bones. During this time of seclusion, the grandmothers and aunts have to teach her two essential things: She must learn the songs to be sung at a funeral so the departed can separate from the village and return home, and she must learn how to have an orgasm. It is believed that without orgasm the sex act cannot invite a child from the other side into the world of the living. To sing the songs of mourning is a woman's sacred duty; the welfare of the ancestors depends on it. To invite life is also a sacred calling, and this a woman does by giving herself over to pleasure.

With initiation sexuality begins moving from the red into "the white." To understand what it means to be erotically in the white, one has to understand a little about Bantu sacred anatomy.

The heart, it is said, is the chief. Should the heart be threatened, then the body itself is endangered, and so the heart is protected by the vigor of the warriors. Anatomically the warriors reside in the solar plexus area. Red sexuality partakes somewhat of the warrior's ambiguous place, neither wild nor domesticated, and its pathologies are often those of gaining or yielding territory. After initiation sexuality lives within the tenderness of two people shaping the sacred space of mutuality.

As in the village, if the chief doesn't draw his wisdom and authority from the domain of the ancestors, he is a charlatan or an egoist.

Karl Laman, in the early twentieth century, interviewed a Bantu Catholic catechist Kunzi about the path of God (nzambi) in the human body. Kunzi claimed that one of God's roads was the spine.

The realm of the ancestors is at the base of the spine and the pelvic cradle: white, cool, that basin of vitality that rises from the depths to enliven and inform the village of the living. It is from the realm of the ancestors that life is ordered and made beautiful, and for the initiated the erotic act both honors that beauty and enacts it, makes it real. To put it another way, one comes into the realm of the sacred in the arms of the beloved. The ancestors and the unborn inspirit the flesh. The circle of eros, ideally, is a generous act of hospitality that the spirits might find a place in the world. Here one is most naked before Spirit. Here the warrior lays down the sword and shield.

Here again, we are speaking of the terrain of initiation, the vivid knowledge that whatever one does in one's life, one is always acting within the invisible enfolded context of the village of the living, ancestors and the unborn. All acts, small and large, have consequences within these enfolded worlds, these worlds are enfolded most intimately into the act of making love. Sexual

violence is violence against all three domains. Tenderness likewise resonates outward in concentric circles towards the past,
in the present moment of the caress and towards the unborn
future. Thus sexuality is a mystery right at the heart of things,
and making love is understood to be involved in the welfare of
the village and the fertility of the land.

It is within this understanding that Mandaza speaks of erotic
intimacy, like friendship, as a matter of serving the spirits of
the beloved. For myself, coming from a culture where intimate
relationships are pinched by measuring what one is or is not
getting out of them, it has been a great relief of stepping into
the selflessness and delight of serving another's spirits. A wide
berth is made for the plurality of the other person, and a certain forgetfulness descends over issues of extracting something
from him or her or disappointment that he or she isn't quite
up to one's standards. There is a yielding to the intentionality of
the other, who sometimes knows more about serving my spirits
than I myself know. The spirits being served come forth and
sustain a friend or a lover. In this manner both humans and
ancestors are sustained in ways that they couldn't conceivably
sustain themselves.

Given the inheritance of American puritanism, the African
understanding of the erotic relationship between soul and Spirit
is likely to sound remote and exotic, but this has to be judged
within a cross-cultural context. Desexualizing Spirit is a decided-
ly minority perspective. In Catholicism, especially the Carmelite
tradition, the soul is the bride of Christ, and the erotic poetry
of St. John of the Cross ranks among the best. In Judaism the
relationship between Israel and God is understood as explicitly
erotic, the mystical text being the Songs of Solomon: "I am black
and comely," declares the King's Ethiopian lover. Orthodox Jews
are called to make love on the Sabbath because that is when
the feminine aspect of God, the Shekinah, comes out of exile
and yields to the embrace of God's masculine presence. One
could make a long list of other examples: the Fravashi in Sufic

Islam also called the spirit of the way; Krishna dancing with the Gopis; the erotic relations between Buddhist and Hindu practitioner with nature spirits, the devas and dakinis, etc. Bantu culture, in other words, participates in a venerable cross-cultural tradition that recognizes spirit longs for soul as surely as soul longs for Spirit.

Mandaza says,

> The water spirits come in the form of a lover or wife because they are flesh and blood. You cannot separate the two. They want to make love, to join together as one thing.

It has been my observation that intimacy with the world of Spirit has all the natural range of any erotic relationship from wild passion to weathered bliss, from tumult to domestic tranquility. The soul can know nothing of its true dimensions except by living through and into an authentic relationship with Spirit. Within the natural range of this relationship, the soul is tempered, softened, as my friend Jay Salter would say, like chewed leather.

During my first initiation I was at the Zambezi with Mandaza. We had spent much of the morning in the river itself, and I was happy to tell Mandaza that the Spirit of the River was coming into focus. In the water I could see the iridescent blue and green jewelry of the Mambokadzi. That afternoon we went into a tourist shop so I could buy a necklace for her for she was now in my body and for me to wear something beautiful was a way to celebrate that we were now together. On display in the store was a T-shirt with an image of a reclining white woman with long flowing blond hair that became the river and ultimately cascaded over a cliff into the very image of Victoria Falls. Beneath the white woman it said simply, "Natural Beauty."

I found this T-shirt deeply offensive. In a black country with no lack of gorgeous African women that this blond white girl would represent "natural beauty" seemed like one of the ugly and insidious ways European fantasies colonize the soul.

Mandaza didn't see at all what I saw for the simple reason that he didn't see an image of a white woman or, for that matter, a human being. "There she is," he said, "that is the one we call Mambokadzi."

Water spirits sometimes come erotically as white "women" and "men." As with the white ngozi, it took me quite a long time to understand that these are in fact spirits, not at all human. Among the Bantu the distinction is clear if only that these lovers quite often come as mermaids or angels in people's dreams and visions. Among American blacks they are marked as spirit by other means: a certain luminosity and unearthliness, the ability to communicate telepathically, a private language, an unusual relationship with water, the capacity to defy gravity.

To write of the erotic image of the white woman (and to a far less degree, the white man) opens up a can of worms that others are better qualified to deal with for she carries desire, danger, transgression, hope and outrage in different ways for black and white men and women. To get entangled in the sexual politics of this seems like a great distraction to me, for "she" is not human; she is an image, an imago, a spirit, a potency that confuses people of both European and African descent with longing and fear. The confusion of longing and fear is already difficult enough to work with without making human what belongs to the realm of spirit.

Calvin C. Hernton's heartbreaking essay on coming of age as a black man in the South gave me a clue to understanding the place where European and African culture overlap that confuses the sexualities of contemporary blacks and whites.

> For the myth of white womanhood has soaked into the Negro's skin. In matters of beauty, manners, social graces, and womanly virtues, the white woman is elevated by American society to the status of a near goddess. Everywhere, the Negro hears about and sees these nymphlike creatures . . . It becomes all but impossible for the black man to separate his view of the ideal woman from that of the white woman.

To lift this out of sexual politics into spiritual longing, the key words are "myth," "goddess," "ideal" and, most importantly, "nymphlike creatures" for nymph is the European name for water spirit.

In Latin, nympha is a nubile young woman. "The same word was applied to female-genital symbols like the lotus flower, water lilies, and certain shells," writes Barbara Walker.

> As spirits of nature, the "nymphs" were believed to embed their souls forever in certain parts of the natural world . . . there were water nymphs, tree nymphs, mountain nymphs, and nymphs who dwelt in the earth, the sea, or Fairyland. Their ancient connection with sexuality was more or less consistently maintained.

The erotic presence of the nymph is ancient. A very direct lineage can be traced through the poetry of Sappho, Roman statuary of the Graces, Botticelli's Venus naked on the half shell all the way to Humbert Humbert, Tinkerbell, Calvin Klein and, God help us, contemporary pornography, which is fond of coupling the white nymphet with the black stud. At its origins this eroticism is profoundly spiritual. In contemporary America, like everything else, it has been trivialized into a commodity (the ultimate commodity) that sells every other conceivable commodity from toothpaste to patriotism. "The Negro's world is thoroughly invaded," Hernton continues, "by the white women. The mass media, newspapers, magazines, radio, and especially television bring these lily white sirens into the blackness of the Negro's home and mind."

In ways that are startling, the traditional European stories of the nymphs parallel fairly exactly the Bantu stories of the water spirits, and given the primordial associations of the water spirits with whiteness, it's entirely possible that these mermaids, as Mandaza calls them, were white before European contact.

It is a contemporary stereotype that make these nymphs slight, sweet, innocent, pretty and without soul. In the old stories, both African and European, these are formidable presences, both kind and uncompromising. They may sometimes giggle like girls, but there is good reason Mandaza uses the honorific "grandmothers" when he speaks of them for they are the oldest and most venerable of the spirits. "It's like in Genesis," Mandaza says, "when the spirit of God moved over the waters. That is when the njusu were born." It is for this reason that in both African and European folklore, the unwary are often pulled down into their secret domain: Ambuya Magumbe having spent so many years living at the bottom of a river, Fata Morgana as a mermaid drawing a sailor to her palace under the sea. Shango's fear was well placed as he and Yemaya drifted from the shore for it is the way of the water spirits to take one down to the very bottom of things and it is in relationship with the water spirits that one enters into a true intimacy with the natural world.

I return now to Teresa, Zora's twin who I mention in Chapter 2. This was one of Teresa's more benevolent dreams:

> I live in the clouds, but I'm swimming in crystal-clear powder blue water though in my waking life I can't swim. I am white, and my hair is very long and blond. Unlike real life, I'm healthy, and everything is great.

In Tommy's dream of being turned white and taken into the family of a white doctor, Mandaza saw witchcraft being performed by people who were masquerading as water spirits. In contrast, Mandaza sees this dream as redemptive:

> This woman is surrounded by very powerful water spirits. They are always around her. In this dream I see no obstacles, but sometimes they are hidden and only become clear after initiation. She becomes a white woman with blond hair; that's a mermaid, to be sure. She is white because she is united with her spirits. She's been transformed. That's why she lives in the clouds like the angels that bring rain.

Phyllis Porter of Arkansas is an artist in her mid-forties, exceptionally skilled in paper and ink, pencil, portraiture. She enjoys illustrating her dreams, and the women in the pictures are often voluptuous. Water is a common theme in many of the dreams she sent me, even those without white water spirits. This is the only erotic dream I received in which the water spirits were men.

> Imagine a round room with a large stained glass dome through which filters rays of colored light. In the middle of the room is a round bed covered in gold. I enter this room with three men. We are all the same golden color. Sensuality prevails, and as I am making love with one of the men, I look into his eyes and see landscapes as though I'm looking west into a desert sunset. I change partners, and this time I see a deep jungle in his eyes. Again I change partners, and this time it's an eight-point star design which shifts into kaleidoscopic patterns. The scene changes, but we are all still gold, and there is no bed in the center but a pool. We all jump in and find we share the waters with sea-horses. We splash and play, and our gold colors dissolve. I am black, and they are red, yellow and white.

"This particular person," says Mandaza,

> is being called by her earth spirits in the jungle and her water spirits, who are coming in different forms. I'd initiate her in water, and I'd take her to holy shrines and teach her how to meditate.
>
> There is in this case the obstacle of the red light. The spirits here are saying we are all still being haunted by this red mark; that is an evil spirit that is haunting the good spirits. After the removal of the red obstacle, the dreamer and her spirits can mate.
>
> The seahorse is a water spirit, and so is the white person even though he has no fins or wings."
>
> These spirits want to get married to the dreamer; that is why they come sexually. She is being initiated into more than one water spirit.

The benevolent circle of initiated sexuality is tainted by the red. Phyllis calls this dream, "It's in the Eyes," and there is some sense that through the eyes of spirit, she draws in the four directions and perhaps the four elements, at least earth and water, and the primary colors as well. As an artist, Phyllis dreams her reconciliation with Spirit as a revelation of beauty, balance and pleasure.

John is a young man I met at a bus stop. Probably in his early twenties, I confess I know little about him beyond this dream that I recorded on a microcassette:

> I was making love with this white woman, and it seemed like after we finish, we was in a circus and we was swinging on the high wire and it broke. But I never ever hit the ground, and I was hollering so loud that I could see everything that was happening in the world, and then it seemed like I was being run over by a cloud in the sky.

"Some of these spirits live in the clouds," comments Mandaza,

> and when you mate with them, you can see all over the earth. It is like this in my own dreams. When I am the white eagle, I can look down and see which fields have received too much rain and which are wanting.

Marcus Bontemps, a citizen of South Central L.A, had the following dream not long after the Los Angeles uprising of 1992:

> The dream began during the riots, but I was carried away in a mist only to be in a foreign land. I meet a Swedish woman on the cobbled streets, and we go for a long walk together. We went up a hill through a lot of flowers and crossed a Japanese bridge over a stream or pond to a little cottage. Here we eat fish and rice, my favorite meal.
>
> Her hair is blond, and her eyes are blue. My skin is very dark, and my hair is a short Afro cut in the latest military style. My friend has an off-yellow thick sweater on and a skirt like the ones Catholic girls wear.
>
> I begin to kiss her hungrily on the neck, and she begins to pull up her sweater. She is so pretty and eager to love me. When I whisper in her ear, she looks at me confused, and I realize that she doesn't understand earthly language. However, we can communicate mind to mind, and she undresses, and we make love.

The next thing I remember is that the both of us are at a chapel getting married. Then the mist gathers again, and she is taken away from me. I'm left screaming and reaching for her, and when I look around, I'm back at my house, and there is rioting outside. I often think what was the meaning of that dream.

Mandaza's answer to Marcus's question is,

This man here has protection from his spirits when others were being arrested and killed. The spirits are saying, "Come to me. I am with you. I'll always be with you." He needs to go back to his spirits. This business of appearing and disappearing in clouds tells me she is a rainmaker. He married that mermaid, but he grieves because he must never let go of his spirits.

This final dream is another I received from homeless Tommy. It is extremely elaborate, being a long post-apocalyptic trek with two water spirits across the sacred river to the House of God. Although it is not an explicitly erotic dream, its mythology is thoroughly Bantu Christian with profound erotic implications. Without a white and oriental water spirit to accompany him, Tommy could never find his way to where God lives.

I was walking through the forest with a white lady and also an oriental lady with short hair. We were searching for the Lord's house just as many others had searched, and we were tired and weary. In the Bible, in Revelations 21, it speaks of God's house; so we searched diligently. After our father Adam died, the Garden of Eden was lost to us humans. We were told that only the righteous could enter the House of God, but no matter how hard we traveled, we could not get close.

I needed the white lady because she carried a grace and mercy I did not possess. And the oriental had a deep strong quietness and a knowledge of medicine and herbs, which was useful for my HIV condition.

In the dream we were nude. We could not wear old clothes because they were stained with old world sins. The white woman carried a basket of food which never ran out. Our water came from a stream that led to the river that came out of God's throne.

Everything around us was so full of color: green of different shades, and there were good vegetables to eat. There were no animals because many had fled inside the New House of God which came down out of the sky for all Godlike people. In God's house everything would be made new, even our bodies. My spear would become a staff like Moses', our father of old. Once inside we would meet Jesus! No more sex with the women on the other side of the river because we would all be united with God. We also left our food on this side of God's river.

The white woman was hated because nobody understood her speech except me and the oriental lady. The oriental lady communicated with me telepathically.

These events took place after 2021 A.D. During 1997, a vaccine was put out that didn't cure AIDS but made death a lot slower. I do not know if we each entered God's house because I woke up before the dream ended.

Knowing Tommy's status as a homeless black man with HIV, Mandaza says,

This man here has been driven into desperation from not having been accepted by the white community; so he suffers from the disease of poverty. If he calls upon his spirits, on God and Christ, he will be free. The white woman is a water spirit with a basket of food that is never empty, and the oriental woman also is a water spirit. He's the only one who can understand what his spirits are saying to him. No other people can understand that.

Who is easier to cast into the trash bin of history than a black madman without a roof over his head? Only he after all can understand what his spirits are saying to him. And yet this dream yields the essential insight into the erotic relationship between soul and Spirit.

The sacred cosmos of the dream is transparently Bantu, and given that Central African people have used the poetic imagery of the Bible to understand their place in the universe for over five centuries, I could as well have come across this dream in Kinshasa or Johannesburg as in Santa Monica.

Consider this song from the Church of the Holy Spirit, Matadi (formerly Zaire), 1971:

> How did the children of Israel cross over?
> By his staff they crossed over
> How did the children of the spirit cross over?
> By the strength of God they crossed over
> I have seen the water they asked for in the house of God
> All those who have received water to drink shall be saved.

The biblical trek from humanity's exile from Eden through a corrupted world across the sacred river to the house of God is reminiscent of the Fu Kiau Bunseki's rendition of the Bakongo myth of exile that "establishes the dominant theme of Kongo religion, wholeness achieved by the union of opposites." Recall that the descendants of Mahungu, the androgynous God, "were decimated, divided and scattered by a flood, a famine and the loss of the sword of chiefship, the source of order. The flood remains in the form of the mythical river nzadi". For traditional Kongolese people, it was said that Mbanza Kongo, the holy city that reflects the undivided wholeness of God was on the other side of Nzadi. For contemporary Kongolese Christians, Mbanza Kongo goes under the Christian name of the New Jerusalem. For Tommy the domain of sacred order across the river from a disordered world is called the House of God.

Bantu Christians have always been close to the figure of Moses, not only because colonialism corralled them into the house of bondage but also because Moses parted the waters. When Tommy says that in the House of God his "spear would become a staff like Moses, our father of old," it's impossible not to see the sword of chiefship passed down from the ancestors. I glance at the ancestor's staff that lies on the table next to me, carved by Mandaza out of the hardwood of a rare tree that carried the power to protect the people from witchcraft and ngozi. This sword, this staff also connects the world of the ancestors to the world of the living.

These Bantu details — Tommy's radical dependence on the water spirits in a long and frustrating pilgrimage, the staff of the ancestor who parted the waters, the sacred river and the sacred world on the other side of it — show how completely intact Africa is in the soul of one black American. But the clincher in terms of the erotic questions in this chapter is expressed in the statement that on the other side of the river, sex would no longer be necessary because "we would all be united with God."

I must invoke again Fu Kiau Bunseki: In the beginning God "divided into two, male and female; unable to reconstitute the original unity, the two reconciled themselves by inventing marriage." We all know what it is to long for God, but who knows how God longs for us, in fact needs us to enact the rites that make God whole? On this side of the river among the living, God expresses this longing through the beloved, human or spirit, that reaches out to us and draws us forth. In the arms of the beloved, God is made whole, and within the intimate embrace one partakes of the wholeness of God. The longing of God draws us across the harsh and perplexing landscape of this life. God's longing is as much a part of the pilgrimage as is our own. Tommy's dream speaks of two ways of sacred knowing, one for one side of the river and one for the other.

> For now we see through a glass, darkly; but then face to face:
> Now I know in part; but then shall I know even as I am known.

No creature ever falls short of its own
completion. Wherever it stands, it does
not fail to cover the ground.

Dogen Zenji

THE SPIRIT OF THE GIFT

CONCLUSION

When I told Mr. Baldwin that I was writing a book about black people's dreams about whites, he said, "I don't think I ever dream about white folks." But a couple of mornings later as I was drawing up another syringe of morphine, he was happy to offer the dream that Mandaza and I claim as our favorite:

> I was back in Louisiana someplace on this farm, and I was on this pole like I was a scarecrow. All the birds was black, and the corn was white. A machine would pick the corn from the field, and I would throw the birds into the machine with the white corn, but behind this machine all these little white babies was being planted. They was being pushed into holes, but I was strapped to my pole, and I was hurt that I could not help these babies.

All of Mandaza's adult life has been involved with the welfare of children, and I think it's safe to say that alongside healing, tending to the little ones is his true love. As a teenager, he was an avid leader in the Boy Scouts, teaching children the stars, the way of the bush and how to care for the old folks. His professional life found him teaching the children of the British South African Police, and for the sheer pleasure of it, he'd often organize evening classes because, as he put it to me, "I loved those little ones." At the time of his sudden retirement, he had been promoted to be in charge of all the police schools in Zimbabwe.

Of Mr. Baldwin's dream, Mandaza says,

> This is a very unique and powerful, a very accommodating dream. The dreamer has a spirit that looks at the world from a very powerful perspective. The spirit wants to feed the world, feed the hungry. This one has got work to look after children. By looking out after the children, he's planting new seeds in the ground.
>
> What resurrects results from the children growing up and making a new world.
>
> The world lives on the corn. It's an evil spirit that makes him reach for the children, a confused act of kindness. He thinks he should rescue the children when he's really preventing them from growing. It is the work of God to plant these children, but he is trying to rescue them! God says, "Why are you not allowing them to be planted in the soil?" Once you remove that spirit, God will help him take care of the next generation.

What is this spirit that would interfere with our children being planted in the soil? And if the children find no place to sink their roots, what harvest will there be, what future? In Mandaza's analysis a key word, thoroughly Bantu and for that reason thoroughly African-American: resurrection. Planting seeds, yes. Harvest, yes. But let us not forget that the new world depends on the resurrection of Spirit and that it is through our children that the resurrection of possibility presents itself most vividly:

> What resurrects results from the children growing up and making a new world.

Let me dance slowly around the essential connection between resurrection and education. I admit it is a strange way to write an essay, this winding of a theme (resurrection/ education) between stories, but I don't know how else to do justice to the Bantu point of view. I'll begin with two stories that from the Bantu perspective overlap though from a contemporary American point of view, they may seem quite different.

When my daughter Nicole was six years old, on the anniversary of my father's death, I went to the ocean with her to scatter a few handfuls of his ashes. As we walked back to the car, I noticed that Nicole was in an unusually reflective mood.

"I never look out over the sea." she said.

"Why is that, Nicole?" I replied.

"I don't think I can tell you," she responded.

I chose not to question her further, but after we walked a ways, she said, "I've decided that when I'm old and it is time to die, then I will look out over the sea."

The second story I'll let James Hillman tell:

> Amateur Night at the Harlem Opera House. A skinny, awkward sixteen-year-old goes fearfully onstage. She is announced to the crowd: "The next contestant is a young lady named Ella Fitzgerald . . . Miss Fitzgerald here is gonna dance for us . . . Hold it, hold it. Now what's your problem, honey? Correction, folks. Miss Fitzgerald has changed her mind. She's not gonna dance, she's gonna sing . . ."
>
> Ella Fitzgerald gave three encores and won first prize. However, she had meant to dance.

The English word education comes from the Latin educere, literally to bring or draw forth. What exactly do we seek to draw forth in our children? What nourishes them, in fact educates them from the root upwards? In Bantu culture, education — bringing, drawing, calling forth — addresses those old spirits that want to come through us to extend their gifts to the community. It is in the awakening of the gift, the nourishing of it, the honor given to the spirit of the gift that brings together education and resurrection, the world of the living and the generosity of the ancestors.

The interaction with Nicole was in no way ordinary between us. I saw other such glimmers perhaps a half a dozen times during her childhood. In America we are likely to call such a child precocious, which often leads us to treat them as precious little ornaments on the parent's narcissism. If they are less fortunate, they will be dismissed or even punished as weird. I do not expect to see the day when what Mandaza would call a grandmother spirit is acknowledged, protected and perhaps drawn forth in an American school.

What or who is it that we draw forth and from where? How do we call out to the spirit of the gift?

In Shona the spirit that came through Ella Fitzgerald when she was a skinny little thing is called a "shave" (pronounced "shavay"). If I were to translate shave, I would call it the spirit of the gift. A musician is said to have a music shave just as a skilled thief or a talented lover are said to have shaves that know the arts of thievery or making love. Such a person is gifted, a gift has been extended to them, or they are vehicles for the spirit of the gift. Just as Mandaza and I initiate people into the ngoma of the water spirits, so do we initiate people into relationship with their shave. (Mandaza also casts out shaves that are troublesome and destructive to the community.)

Mandaza says, "

> A good shave brings not only prosperity but gifts such as poetry, mbira, dance and so forth. If you resist such a shave, it's as if you are saying to God, "Get out of my way!" If you resist the gift that the shave offers to you, the spirit will disappear. The shave will say, "He is resisting me. I will leave and find someone else." The shave may be invited by good spirits that are upon someone else, and with those spirits it will find a home.
>
> To be initiated, you learn how to serve the shave. For example, the spirit might say I want you to have a walking stick to take with you wherever you go or mbira, or when the shave is with you, it takes snuff. It is not you taking the snuff; it is the shave. It is his food.
>
> When a musician has a guitar or mbira, it belongs to the shave, not to the person. When a musician who is initiated picks up the mbira, it is also the shave who is picking it up. You are trance possessed by the shave as you play mbira. And what do you find? The audience is excited, and they throw gifts at you,

but they are really throwing gifts to the shave.

One can say the same about a writer who picks up a pen.

There are also shave that heal. It can even show you herbs. Some shave can heal with touch or with water.

It is not only the shave who picks up the musical instrument or the pen or who heals. It may also be one of your ancestors. The ancestors and the shave work together.

Shaves often appear suddenly: Ella onstage belting out the spirit of song. Mandaza tells his equivalent of Ella's story in TWIN OF ANOTHER TRIBE.

One time — I think I was probably under ten years of age — my uncle was hit by a lightening bolt that came with the rain, and his hand was curled up like a chicken foot. My elder aunt was there with her daughter, crying, looking at my uncle. He was lying there, and they couldn't do anything. So I went into the bush and brought some fiber from a tree and tied it with a stick like a splint, opening his hand and fingers, tying the stick up to his elbow. After two days it healed. He was able to spread his fingers. That was my first experience as a healer.

Shave are always on the lookout for windows of opportunity to come into the human world, and children are especially susceptible to the spirit of the gift. When my brother Eugene was about seven years old, his favorite activity was to sit along the street we lived on with his eyes closed and listen to the passage of cars. Eugene had the uncanny ability to distinguish the different kinds of cars by the sounds they made. Perhaps in another era he would be listening to the sounds of the forest, and his parents might think a hunting shave was at work. It is not surprising that in Eugene's case he grew up to be a musician.

Windows of opportunity. The shave wants in. I remember sitting under a mountain lilac with my granddaughter Jamie when she was four. Jamie started pulling leaves off the tree. I winced at my lack of words for why that was no way to treat a living being until I remembered Grandmother Willow, the ambuya spirit in Walt Disney's POCAHANTAS, who imparts her wisdom to the young squaw. Jamie got it immediately. A couple of years later, I began to teach her the wild herbs I learned when I was a child and how to ask permission of the plant before one picks horsetail, wild strawberry, burdock, blessed thistle, salsify.

> "Look here, Jamie, this is yarrow. In China they dry out the stalks and throw them on the ground to talk to God."
> "Really?"
> "It's a known fact. And this plant here is called plantain. We use it in the hospital. If you can't poop, you grind up the seeds and mix them with juice, and then you will be able to poop without any problem at all!"

I would not guarantee that Jamie becomes the first nganga of Alpha, New Jersey. Few things in life are so predictable. False starts are the routine. My friend Allan Brill, for example, was sure he was fated to be a professional baseball player until the terrible afternoon when he didn't make the seventh grade team. Instead he ultimately became a union organizer, a virtuoso union organizer. As Leonard Cohen sings, "Bless the continuous stutter of the word as it turns into flesh." Jamie may not become a nganga, but there is always hope for the future of intelligent life in America when a shave can even slide past the banality of Disney to enliven the imagination.

The shave is about the word becoming flesh, nothing less. Spirit wants to move. It wants to move in and through the community. The gift wants to be passed on. Spike Lee's remarkable film HE GOT GAME can be read as a praise song to the spirit of the gift and as a morality tale about how one carries the gift in a culture maddened by money.

"Basketball is poetry in motion," says the teenage protagonist Jesus Shuttlesworth. This poetry, this shave that needs to be enacted was Jesus' inheritance from his not-so-heavenly father Jake, who on one hand nourished and fiercely challenged his son's talents throughout his childhood and on the other inadvertently killed Jesus' mother in his son's presence.

Within these circumstances Lee frames a drama that is part Christ's temptation in the wilderness and part Bantu initiation ritual. As is commonly the case in West African stories, Jake is tricked into ritual circumstance — in this case into helping initiate the son who despises him. The governor arranges that Jake be let out of prison briefly with the promise of early parole if he can convince his son to play for the governor's favorite team.

Jesus has a couple of days to decide what he is going to do with his gift, with his life. High school is over, professional teams are offering him vast amounts of money, college teams ply white women on him. Friends and relatives and hordes of strangers, attracted to the aura of celebrity, all want a piece of him. HE GOT GAME is, among other things, a relentless study of American demonology, and true to Lee's wild democratic vision, demons of every race, class and gender tempt Jesus in the wilderness of initiation.

This is the bush of ghosts beyond the edge of the village, beyond the range of what was once familiar. Those who have been initiated know this wilderness well, and it is nothing less than merciless. Jesus is at the crossroads, and in the chaotic swirl of choice, he has to ask what it is that he serves with his life. He turns to what in Africa would be called an ancestors' altar — photographs and old letters from his mother. Her voice is clear, translucent amid so many conflicting voices: Get an education. The gift requires a life that can carry it; without that life the gift will destroy you.

Jake's reappearance deepens and thickens his son's chaos, and the ethical burden lies on his (Jake's) shoulders. His mojo rests in the gospel of forgiveness. In prison he accepted Christ and yielded to being forgiven for the violence he had done. He also accepted a brief furlough from prison with the possibility of release if he convinced his son to play on the governor's team. His temptation is no less fierce than Jesus'. He cannot coerce his son even if it means spending several more years behind bars. If Jake is not impeccable, if he doesn't carry the role of the elder, his son's soul might well be lost in the bush of ghosts. Between his mother on the other side and his father, who is all too alive, Jesus must choose his fate.

It would be unkind to reveal the end of the story, but it's worth mentioning that Lee embeds another and essential Bantu detail in his film. In Bantu culture, the blessing of the father is extremely powerful. To leave home, to make a life for oneself without being blessed by the father or, worse yet, to be followed by the father's curse is a terrible thing and often leads towards all manner of mishap and catastrophe. Here one can see the full complexity of Jesus' shave initiation for he cannot give himself over to the spirit of the gift without being aligned with his mother's wisdom and blessed by his father's good wishes. The final confrontation leaves father and son at the crossroads, on the basketball court where Jesus defeats his father with fury and Jake plays the initiator, who is also the trickster. As he's escorted away from his son back to prison, he levels with the final words of a man who knows what it is to be undone by rage.

"You look out for yourself. You look out for your sister. You ain't got to worry about me no more, but you get that hatred out of your heart, boy, or you're going to end up just another nigger like your father. It's your ball." Jesus received the shave spirit through his father, and his father, defeated, leaves with his son the holy riddle of the trickster. It is up to Jesus whether these words be a blessing or a curse.

When being initiated, the spirits come forth illuminating the terrain of an inspirited life and asking the questions that cut to the heart of what it means to live such a life. HE GOT GAME says quite a lot about the spirit of the gift that resonates with a nganga's work with shave spirits.

The gift carries heat. It generates its own fire. To burn with the gift is extraordinary, as if one becomes, momentarily, the burning bush that astonished Moses. But in African medicine the subtle work of initiation requires the tempering of fire so that it is carried deeply and one is not undone by the volatility of the spirit. Throughout West and Central Africa, one calls on the female spirits to cool the fire. In Lee's movie Jesus' mother carried that coolness while his father fanned the flames. Working with shave requires both.

Within what life will you shelter the gift? So asks the mother. The uninitiated may not know that the gift needs to be sheltered. The deliberate and painstaking work of building a house for the spirit, making one's life a hospitable place for spirit to inhabit, is a labor that for many people does not come easy.

The spirit seeks and needs its sacred niche and requires its sacred instruments. The basketball court is such a niche, the basketball such an instrument. Someone with a writing shave could say the same about pen and paper. Without the niche and without the required instrument, the fire of the shave cannot flare forth nor can it be skillfully contained. With niche and instrument, one is ritually prepared to call forth the spirit.

The shave needs a village. This is very important, and in a world that is more interested in commodities than gifts, it is routinely the source of great confusion and not rarely, self-destruction. A village is not an audience. The ego may want an audience to applaud its magnificence, but ego gets in the way of the spirit coming through. The tightrope between ego and shave is the same as between greed and generosity. One presumes that at his lucid best, Jesus knows that he is offering the village the poetry in motion that is basketball. When he is faithful to the poetry, the shave will come through generously. If the same poetry becomes a praise song to his ego, then he dishonors spirit and dishonors the village. Moreover, he has sold his soul before even having a chance to know its dimensions.

Lee's movie engaged the critical question, the one question that clarifies one's relationship to the gift and in so doing brings one's life into order: What is the gift for?

Mandaza and I once tried to initiate a man whose situation was virtually the Shona version of Jesus Shuttleworth's. I will call him Josiah.

Like Jesus, Josiah's gift was recognized when he was a boy, the gift of playing mbira, the thumb piano that calls forth the spirits but which among Bantu people is also enjoyed for its mere beauty. By the time Josiah was thirteen, he was dressed like a girl so he could sneak past soldiers and into the bush to play mbira for the guerillas.

When Josiah came to be healed by Mandaza and myself, he was in his late twenties, and mbira was simultaneously all he lived for and the source of bitter affliction. From the time he was a child, he had been pressured to become a trance medium, a position that carried enormous responsibilities that he wanted nothing to do with. He knew that those who wanted him to walk that path had their own ambitions, most notably prestige and money. A modest fame had given him a ticket to America and a possibility of escaping the poverty of the township. It also brought him money, the envy and enmity of kin, two white girlfriends, a death threat, a confused incapacity to tell truth from lying, and a hex from his older sister that delivered Josiah to the ranks of the walking dead. Even still, when he played mbira, grown men, or at least Mandaza and I, would weep.

Although his shave was quintessentially Shona, Josiah had come to despise traditional Bantu culture and had embraced the pure land Buddhism of one of his American girlfriends. Whatever medicine Mandaza and I did on his behalf had to be strictly minimalistic. Mandaza worked with herbs and immersion in water, and I worked with the cards and the Japanese chant "nam myo ho renge kyo."

Josiah was as lost in the bush of ghosts as anyone I have ever met, and so we invoked the spirit of mbira as a presence that could help him find his way through the wilderness. Only one question was relevant, and I had him play out that question on the mbira itself: to whom do I play? As he played, I drew a card on his behalf without turning it over, and when he finished, I asked him who he saw.

"The Rainmaker is who I play to." he said with a glow on his face that surprised me. He never knew whom he was playing for. He thought it was for the audiences.

I turned over the card: the Emperor. Zeus, father of the gods who bears the Word that brings order to a disordered world; in one hand the earth, in the other a fistful of lightening and on his shoulder a bird that Josiah recognized from his childhood — Chapungu, the black eagle. Josiah wept a little and even laughed.

"Is it? I play mbira for God?"

"Exactly."

And so the father's blessings were imparted on Josiah, perhaps prematurely for he is not out of the woods yet. Armed with only his mbira and "nam myo ho renge kyo." he was taught to call on Spirit when he is overwhelmed with confusion. Without question, crossing the river will be bitter for Josiah, and we pray that he survives the passage.

Calling forth the spirits — the spirit of the gift, the ancestors — is a political act; one might say in a disinspirited world, it is the essential political act. At one point Josiah, much to his surprise, was trance possessed by an old mbira player that Mandaza recognized immediately as pre-colonial, that is to say, from before the whites defeated the Shona and the Ndebele in the 1890's. Such spirits are rare, but we're watching them rise up with more frequency, perhaps attracted to the spectacle of a white and black man practicing medicine together. "It's just as our Grandmother Nehanda said when the whites hung her by her neck: 'My bones will rise.' This is what is happening," says Mandaza.

Earlier I said that in Bantu medicine healing is about removing the obstacles so that Spirit can move through a broken world — this body, this family, this community — and make it whole. Strictly speaking, this is about the resurrection of the dead. Call and response — the Bible cries out, "Son of Man, can these bones live?"

And Ambuya Nehanda responds, "My bones will rise."

Calling forth Spirit. Gathering in Spirit. Letting God breathe on dry bones. Letting the little child lead us to the Promised Land. On this note I will leave the reader with Mandaza's final words on living in an inspirited world:

> Remember we've got earth spirits, we've got water spirits, we've got air spirits, we've got spirits of fire. They come in different forms.
>
> Earth spirits can come in the form of black people. Earth spirits are actually the spirits put on earth by God. They own the riches beneath the earth; they own the power to heal. They have the full balance. Lions, Rhino, Elephant, Buffalo, the Chapungu — these are earth spirits. They say, "Respect the earth because it is a home for the Creator."
>
> Fire spirits are the warriors. For them red is not an evil color. They bring fire to burn out the rubbish. And when the rubbish is burned, it turns into water.
>
> I work with everything, not only water, because my spirits need balance. We must be balanced. I find balance with honoring water and earth below, the Universe above. If one side of the triangle is not there, things are unbalanced.
>
> What we do here is not about changing culture; it is about bringing people to the world of the spirits, about making the connection between people and the natural world. People are always eager to change culture, to improve it, but look now at the chaos and confusion and misery. Now that the old world is almost finished with, are we happy? Yes, people can change a culture into an evil thing by their greed and desires; so we must find our way to the real culture — the earth culture, the water culture, the culture of the Universe. The way of the spirits is in the balance of that sacred triangle.
>
> The spirits come in our dreams and tell us how to walk this path. When I look at these dreams you read me of black Americans, they are exactly the same as my people. The differences are only created by those who interpret the dreams to fit

their own situation. If you interpret dreams that way, you will get lost. The dreams will only confuse you. But if we ask the spirits to interpret the dreams for us, then we can fully understand the similarities between the spirit world of black Americans and black Africans.

The original spirit that lives in the earth and the water and the Universe remain with all of us of African descent. You ask me how this can be, but you already know the answer to that question, mapatya. The African spirits came to America with the slaves. Even after hundreds of years, the spirits have kept faith with their children.

THIS BODY, THIS VILLAGE, THIS MEDICINE

(for Mandaza Kandemwa)

The spider's touch, how exquisitely fine!
Feels at each thread and lives along the line.

Alexander Pope

1.

Held in palm
Medicine bundle
Spider beaded to soft leather

"It is she who sent me to Africa"
I said, "She who
makes the connections."

Flat amethyst
Herb damp with oil
    and an old man's sweat

2.

"Typical water spirit person,"
    said the nganga.
"Your story is mine.

Fatherless. War. Hunger.
Most nearly mad with heartbreak.

161

And like me you came to your enemy
    to be initiated."

3.

Spider weaves her web star by star
as the sun darkens
hunts all night
eats tattered web
one star at a time
as the sun rises

Through the cold dark
ancestors hold council
around small fires the world over

Mist and smoke at the thin horizon

The world is endangered, brother.
Not just that small tribe
of crazed monkies
that call themselves human
but all that they would devour

With the rising of the sun
the twilight of the gods

Weaving
Unweaving
And perhaps reweaving

4.

Illness seeps deep
from an anguished world
birth between bones
crackling of nerves

love, terror and hope

How can it be that this illness
you call water spirit disease
is the presence and wisdom
of the Invisible,

the name of the Nameless God?

5.

Weaving.

The Zambezi so many years ago
web draped on dry bough
laid an altar
in flowers
and elephant dung
sang to the Mother of Water
that she might run in your veins

And so she came
And so the warrior came.
wings wide and riding thermals
And so came the old healer
   his twisted spine
   your body hunched
   around his wound
Spirit after spirit possessing
they took your body
and completed my initiation

Weeping under the Spider web

"There is no cure for
the arrogance of a young man
except time."

And you replied,
"Many have tried
to call these spirits into me
but my ancestors smelled arrogance
and turned away.
You were the first
to approach without
arrogance.

Apartheid between us is over.

colonialism and racism
belong to
    the rubbish bin."

Weaving.

It was then we began
to call each other twin.

mapatya.

6.

Unweaving.
One country
    obscenely wealthy
    would steal food from a child

A village idiot
    coronates himself King.
    Or President.
    Or antichrist
Makes war.
Makes money.
Prays loudly but to whom?

Another country
    obscenely poor

hungers for the salt of God's tears
and a little bread

AIDS filling the City of the Dead
with children

7.

And I lie in bed
sleepless, raving,
urinating on myself,

and again how is it
that Spirit plants medicine
in the body through illness?

multiple sclerosis

How is it that illness itself
Speaks wisdom
dares say the Name
of the god that
   reweaves the world?

8.

Bless my brother's life,
   seed in pink womb sprouting
   to this breath
   to this last breath
   death awakening this blessed life
Bless he who cried to the ancestors,
   "Make this man a healer"
   Who cried again
   "May the way of the peacemaker
   pulse under white skin in Africa
   black skin, America

Bless his life
    brief as heat lightening
    in a time of no rain

9.

You tell me
in a gathering of shamans
no less

"Michael it is time you sing
of how your body
has become medicine."

I trust now
only what is small and true
the soft touch of the hand
the sudden light of the eyes
the impulse of the gut
    toward compassion

Love is the only medicine
I know
and I know it is not mine
passed swift from Lover to Beloved
a gift given and offered
unpossessed
never owned

utterly ordinary

but then, also,
perhaps a song
to those spirits who know
what healing is

as I most certainly do not

10.

the Lover it seems
feeds on suffering
and of that the world in generous

pray to that which has
made my life common and kind

that changes wine to water
not water to wine

for when we refuse the common fate
we become thieves in the night
too dark to ourselves
to see we are thieves

or blinded by light
staggering
unable to see that we blind.

11.

So first before
the legs start giving away
    before I start forgetting
            the English language
    light sucked from me

    eyes dim can
    no longer discern
    the mind of my kin

    wife beside me
    twin

    ten thousand miles away

The body lost, stuttering
    falling again and again
drooling, beshitting myself

Love is the only medicine
    I have ever known
Have ever known

Love cut for the harvest

at last real in its own defeat

12.

We so large and stupid
give the entangled hearts
to the waters of forgiveness

Spider never gets caught
in her own web

13.

So long in the dark
    the stars hatch
    the sac breaks open

are we not born out of our stories?

little spiders
catch the wind with a thread
a wisp
a single hallelujah

You in America
Me in Africa

the old web breaking down
in Spider's belly

cast fresh
with a fresh life

14.

And you mukoma?

With those Africans
    some call American
With those Europeans
    some call American
With those Native people
    off the coast of Canada

The little spider has gone far
has he not?
Born from a story
that we shared
and from which we are delivered

What now can I possibly say?

    In a thousand languages
there is only one word

Notenda, mukoma

saybonile!

gracias a su vida y nuestra vida

Thank you for this life

That prayer

That shuttle

Alone

Sufficient.

       Amen

                    Kasane, Botswana,
                    September 2005

Appendix 1

Many Mansions

When I was recording Mandaza's interpretations of African-American dreams, the question of Christianity came up. As the author this was critical, knowing that most black Americans are Christian or are of Christian background. I felt a need to make this book relevant to them, establishing the profound connections between Afro-Christian tradition and the way of the water spirits.

Mandaza and I have been very much shaped by Christianity, and our work as ngangas reflects this. Once Mandaza told me that when he uses English, he often relies on biblical understandings to explain the way of the spirits, but when he uses Shona, he relies on the old proverbs that carry the wisdom of the ancestors. As for myself, I was raised Catholic/Buddhist and spent a few passionate months as a Pentecostal evangelist when I was fourteen. Christian and Jewish scripture will always be a primary source from which I live my ethical and spiritual life.

And yet neither Mandaza and I are Christians or, for that matter, Christianizable. In Zimbabwe, Christianity is often a dangerous rogue force sowing chaos and destroying families and traditions to erect the edifice of the New Covenant. In bitter moments I sometimes think that the mythic Antichrist is the one who kills Christ in the name of Christ. As ngangas, like it or not, we are on the battlefield — a disturbing struggle on behalf of a sacred tradition, especially for two ragged warriors who are unashamed of our love for Christ. My own naive hope is that someday Christianity will renounce its imperial inheritance and embrace the gospel without prejudice towards traditions that have gospels of their own.

Because this brief conversation about Christianity determined the underlying structure of this book, I record it here for the reader's edification. Mandaza and I on some essential points were in disagreement, and I chose, without dishonoring my mapatya, to take a path that I thought would be most useful to African Americans.

> Michael: I think what happens in America is that people are initiated into water spirits by Christianity. They confess their sins and then are baptized in water.

> Mandaza: That's not true. That's a different initiation, that one. Many people believe that by being a Christian, one is freed. There are so many Christians that are haunted by spirits. They end up leaving the churches to look for other means so that witches and avenging spirits can be chased away from them.

> Michael: When I was a Pentecostal, there were people who had the power of healing who cast out spirits. People would confess their sins and go into the water. They were doing things very similar to ngangas.

> Mandaza: It depends on the power of the person who is initiating. Some spirits pretend. They say, "You have chased me away," but they are lying. I have come across spirits like that here, but when they come to the real power that can cast them out, they confess.
>
> We have got people who have joined churches because they are being haunted by spirits. They thought they were going to be freed in those churches. But what do we find? They are still haunted by these spirits; so in the end they come to the ngangas.

> Michael: Let's presume there was an Apostolic Christian who is filled with the Holy Spirit and by that power he really can cast

out spirits. Then the person does confess and goes into the water. Would you say that there are Apostolics who, even though they don't practice the traditional way, are nonetheless very effective?

Mandaza: I haven't come across such a person in my life. I wandered for many years trying to get help from these people when I was afflicted, but I didn't get anything at all. If there is one person like that, I will say, "Well done," to him. He has my honor and my respect.

Michael: This is a very deep dilemma for African Americans because almost all of them are Christians.

Mandaza: If an Apostolic prophet has worked on somebody, we must see the good results. If he has done his work and the person still suffers, what has been done? We want to see the results, not temporary results, permanent results. "By their fruit ye shall know them."

Michael: I'm not a Christian either. I'm just aware that some of the people who will read this book will be African Americans who have very little connection with traditional African culture and many will be practicing Christians. So I'm trying to understand how to make a bridge between the lives they actually live and how they can be spiritually protected and initiated even as Christians.

Mandaza: I don't believe in Christ. Christ himself said, "Do not call me good master." I believe in the message he brought. He is like the other messengers of God — Abraham, Moses, the other prophets and so forth.

The most important thing here is not to honor the African way of living or the European way of living but to understand what God wants us to do. Whether we call him God or Allah or whether we meet him in a tree — it's the message that counts.

If people are Christians and they submit to God, then God will teach them to heal because God's people are suffering in this world. Healing comes through those who give themselves to God, not those who say, "I pray Mohammed," "I pray Jesus," "I pray

Peter," but who say, "What does God want us to do?"

I look at the world, and I see it has a terrible wound which is bleeding because a particular religion, a particular group of people believe in their own little master. I call them little masters because they have no power over God.

"I am a Christian," "I am Muslim," "I am a Jew" — whatever you call it, that is unimportant. That is irrelevant. Let us look at the one who sent Mahatma Gandhi with a message. Let us look to the one who sent Christ or Nelson Mandela. What does he want us to do? He wants the truth and love. People get distracted by their beliefs and don't pay attention to God. They shout, "I am a Christian," in the streets and know nothing about Christ. This is a disease. That is my personal opinion.

Michael: So it's as Christ said, "In my Father's house, there are many mansions."

Mandaza: Exactly. Christianity is a language to pray to God in, just as Islam is. But God is not a Christian. God is not a Muslim. He has no religion at all. God is just God. "I am that which I am."

Appendix 2

ANOTHER THREAD IN THE RAGGED WEAVE

Every time I try to imagine the life of William Halbert, my mind runs mad with accusation and lament, then goes numb and silent. So I try again.

William Anson Halbert. Red beard, blue eyes, stout, fought in the Virginia Militia in the War of Independence. 1st Regiment, Light Dragoons. For his service, Thomas Jefferson gave him 486 acres on Russel Creek in South Carolina.

He was a pious man, no doubt about it, and very much a man of means. A couple of weeks after Abraham Lincoln's birth, March 5, 1809, "knowing that it is appointed for all men once to die", he commended his soul to the hands of Almighty God, his body to the earth and "the worldly estate it has pleased God to bless me with" he disposed to his beloved wife Elizabeth Hill Halbert, his children and grandchildren.

To Elizabeth "two hundred acres of land, including the plantation whereon now I live, also my household furniture with all my stock of old negroes and other stock of all hinds during her natural life of widowhood."

Some of the Negroes had names. With his coming of age, son Joel got Sal and Mose, Enos got Reda, James got "one young Negro, vis Peter and all the others I gave or put in his possession." Daughters Martha, Mary and Lucinda got a couple of nameless Negroes each along with horses, saddles and furniture.

God had apparently blessed William Halbert with quite a lot of Negroes to be bred alongside the other stock for the next three generations until emancipation. Wealth, one hopes, generates wealth.

Let's fast-forward now a few generations. Best I can tell, my grandfather Herbert Hill was the great great great great grandson of Halbert's brother-in-law the Reverend William Hill, also pious and having a plantation of his own. But Herbert was born to the zinc and copper mines of Magdalena, New Mexico, fathered my father Milford and then Tommy with my white grandmother Lorena, got wild or desperate with the Depression. Lorena used to say he was shot escaping from prison but truth is we know nothing of his fate.

"Your children will never be accepted by either side of the family," wrote Lorena to my father when he married Adelina, my Mexican mother. In fact, the six of us were freely accepted by my Latino kin. Ordinary American mongrels, or "coyotes" as we were called in New Mexico. White kids who are nonetheless Mexican. Mexicans who are quite obviously white.

Lorena got Jesus and got remarried, and in her later years got remarried again to a Mr. Tidwell. Tidwell nursed her as Alzheimers ate away at her brain. Rumor was that he was a proud member of the Ku Klux Klan but truth is we know only that he was a stone cold racist.

Family. Familia.

A month before my father died of alcoholism, his final exchange with Lorena ended, "You have never understood me." And indeed, how could she? He'd declared himself Alamogordo's first Buddhist when he was fourteen, was a self-taught intellectual, agreed to raise his children Catholic, was rather more compelled by Lao Tzu than Billy Graham. Praises be to his drunken Buddhist soul, he broke ranks and he paid the price. Paying the price he left a legacy to his children more generous than that left to him.

To trace then a little bit of the procession of the ancestors in my own body. I have known my father's bitter despair, the raw truths he could never shake, the refuge of the bottle. And

Herbert's vagrant, furtive mind I knew the years I was homeless, mercifully in jail only twice, a lousy thief, a bad boy.

And William Halbert? I know him more intimately than I easily admit. My spiritual life these past thirty years has meant nothing at all if it hasn't been about the melting of the interlard-ed layers of arrogance and rectitude, greed sanctified by Divine Right and the impulse "to keep it or them all under control" - my own demons or whoever else might disturb my complacency.

We all recognize William Halbert, do we not? On the eve-ning news, Senator Halbert, President Halbert. Or perhaps, God forbid, from our own lips we rely on the received clichés say-ing thanks for the worldly estate it has pleased God to bless America with, our eyes blind to the worlds of suffering that make our consumer smorgasbord possible. Two and a half bil-lion people live on less than two dollars a day. The plantation has gone global. We all know that. (Don't we?)

I knew nothing of my slave owning ancestors when I first began being initiated as a nganga (a medicine man) among Bantu folk in Central Africa. I had spent years studying the transformation of Bantu village culture this side of the Atlantic into African-American culture, and I knew South Carolina to be one of the beachheads of the forced migration of Central African people. When I read about Sal and Mose and Reda and Peter, when I meet black Americans named Hill, when I think of the Shona and Ndebele tribes people who affectionately call me twin brother the ambiguity is familiar. I am a white boy who has been received as African. An African who is quite obviously white.

When I arrived in Zimbabwe for my third initiation into the ngoma of the water spirits, I was in a truly foul state of mind, finding little humor that I had made a formidable nganga Mandaza Kandemwa, answerable to the I.R.S. in order to keep our non-profit on the level. The idiot snarls of cross-cultural mis-communication were wearing on both of us. But what to do? A quarter of the tribe has HIV and starvation is a bleak reality.

Mandaza has known racism raw and ugly — the plantation system that was white ruled Rhodesia, the bloodshed of the civil war, the lingering, desperate inequalities. That afternoon he gave me his special snuff ("It cuts through all obstacles") and told me to walk the line between the anguish of the slaves and the blindness of the slaveholders while his spirits searched for that fork in the path whey my ancestors went astray. Some imagine the soul tainted forever by original sin. In spite of apartheid Mandaza sees original innocence as the truth from which one heals.

How much we want our ancestors to be noble, to ennoble us with their greatness, or failing that to be decently anonymous, rising in time and disappearing wave after wave. But ultimately the point seems to be that each of us is an ancestor to the unborn, each a thread in the ragged weave. What will we offer those who will survive us? Their children? Their grandchildren?

I think I must offer a little post script to this appendix. As I write this, 12,000 Somalis are being relocated to America, 120 to Edisto Island where Halbert had his plantation.

Edisto is one of the Bantu beach heads in the United States, the Gullah people (from "Angola") keeping faith these centuries with the ways of the Motherland to a measure exceedingly rare in America.

And the Somalis? Well they are "heathens" from the south of that benighted country, bought and sold as slaves by the Muslim north. Dirt poor. Without English. Having never seen a refrigerator or an indoor bathroom. Unable to drive.

But, praise God, no longer slaves.

GLOSSARY OF BANTU TERMS

AMBUYA
Literally, "grandmother," a Shona term of respect for the oldest and wisest of the feminine spirits.

CHAPUNGU
The King/eagle spirit greatly honored by Shona people as both a warrior and a peacemaker.

KALUNGA
A Kikongo word meaning, variously, God, ocean and the place where the ancestors live. The kalunga line is the mysterious boundary that separates the visible from the invisible worlds.

KUMFINDA
Kikongo; literally, "in the forest." The domain of the ancestors.

MAMBOKADZI
Shona; literally, the Queen. She is the mother of the water spirits and the feminine face of God. "She is the moon, and the stars are her children," says Mandaza. Shona and Ndebele people also associate her with the Blessed Virgin Mary and mother elephants.

MPEMBA

Kikongo word for the place of the ancestors. Also the white kaolin clay at the bottom of rivers that is used in rites of initiation. In contemporary Kongo Christianity, mpemba has become the word for heaven.

NDOKI

In Kikongo, ndoki is the intent to draw power to oneself to be effective in the world. Witches, bandoki, have amplified this individualism to the point of breaking rank with the reciprocities of community life.

NGANGA

A traditional healer, a medicine man or woman.

NGOMA

Literally, drum or drumming. An ancient Bantu way of healing and initiation. In ngoma the patient is afflicted by the ancestors and can only be healed by surrendering to their desire to inspirit the community through him or her. Ngoma diseases are, in other words, calls to initiation.

NGOZI

Shona: spirits seeking justice, usually having been murdered or having committed suicide or otherwise cut down before a full life was lived. Ngozi can cause mental and physical anguish and even death.

NJUZU

Shona: the water spirits. These are spirits of healing and peace-making that are regarded as God's closest allies. The primary ritual of the ngoma of the water spirits is full immersion baptism, which became the primary ritual of African-American culture. In Zimbabwe, they are often seen as angels or mermaids.

NKISI

A Kikongo word meaning both the oldest of the ancestors (those incarnate in the natural world of herbs, stones, shells, etc.) and the small medicine bundles used for protection from whatever might assault the integrity of the soul. Robert Farris Thompson and Fu Kiau Bunseki have demonstrated the direct connection between nkisi and the "mojo" or "hands" assembled by African-American root doctors.

SHAVE

Shona: the "spirit of the gift," which inspirits a "gifted" person. Shave literally means "wandering" in Shona. Butterflies are called "shave shave," and it is felt that these spirits alight on those who will receive them and go elsewhere if they are not made welcome.

BIBLIOGRAPHY

Cohen, Leonard and Sharon Robinson (1988) "Everybody Knows," Stranger Music Inc. (BMI) and Robinhill Music (ASCAP).

Curtain, Philip C. (1969) THE ATLANTIC SLAVE TRADE: A CENSUS. Madison: University of Wisconsin Press.

Gleason, Judith. (1987) OYA: IN PRAISE OF AN AFRICAN GODDESS. New York: Harpers San Francisco.

Gomez, Michael Angelo (1998) EXCHANGING OUR COUNTRY MARKS: THE TRANSFORMATION OF AFRICAN IDENTITIES IN THE COLONIAL AND ANTEBELLUM SOUTH. Chapel Hill, NC: University of North Carolina Press.

Hernton, Calvin C. (1965) SEX AND RACISM IN AMERICA. New York: Anchor Books.

Herskovits, Melville J. (1958) THE MYTH OF THE NEGRO PAST. Boston: Beacon Press.

Higginson, Thomas Wentworth. (1867) "Negro Spirituals." ATLANTIC MONTHLY 19.

Hill, Michael Ortiz and Kandemwa, Augustine. (2002) GATHERING IN THE NAMES: A JOURNEY INTO THE LAND OF AFRICAN GODS. Woodstock, Conn.: Spring Journal Books.

Hillman, James. (1999) THE FORCE OF CHARACTER AND THE LASTING LIFE. New York: Random House.

Hooks, Bell. (1975) BLACK LOOKS: RACE AND REPRESENTA-TION. Boston: South End Press.

Janzen, John M. and MacGaffey, Wyatt. (1974) AN ANTHOL-OGY OF KONGO RELIGION: PRIMARY TEXTS FROM LOWER ZAIRE. Lawrence, Kan.: University of Kansas Publications in Anthropology.

Kazin, Alfred, ed. (1968) THE PORTABLE BLAKE. New York: Viking Press.

MacGaffey, Wyatt. (1986) RELIGION AND SOCIETY IN CEN-TRAL AFRICA. Chicago: University of Chicago Press.

Major, Clarence, ed. (1994) JUBA TO JIVE: THE DICTIONARY OF AFRICAN-AMERICAN SLANG. New York: Penguin Books.

Malcolm X. (1977) THE AUTOBIOGRAPHY OF MALCOLM X AS TOLD TO ALEX HALEY. New York: Ballantine Books.

Morrison, Toni. (1987) BELOVED. New York: Alfred. A. Knopf.

Olli, Alho. (1976) THE RELIGION OF THE SLAVES: A STUDY OF THE RELIGIOUS TRADITION AND BEHAVIOUR OF PLANTATION SLAVES IN THE UNITED STATES 1830-1865. Helsinki: Suoma-lainen Tiedeakatema, Academia Scientiarum Fennica.

SLAVE NARRATIVES FROM MISSISSIPI. WPA Records, 1934.

Thompson, Robert Farris. (1984) FLASH OF THE SPIRIT: AFRICAN AND AFRO-AMERICAN ART AND PHILOSOPHY. New York: Vintage Books.

Thornton, John. (1992) AFRICA AND AFRICANS IN THE MAK-ING OF THE ATLANTIC WORLD 1400-1680. Cambridge, Mass.: Cambridge University Press.

Trump, Donald J. with Schwartz, Tony. (1987) TRUMP: THE ART OF THE DEAL. New York: Ballantine.

Vass, Winifred Kellersberger. (1979) THE BANTU HERITAGE OF THE UNITED STATES. Los Angeles: Center for Afro-American Studies, Univerity of California.

Walker, Alice. (1989) THE TEMPLE OF MY FAMILIAR. New York: Simon and Schuster.

Walker, Barbara G. (1983) THE WOMEN'S ENCYCLOPEDIA OF MYTHS AND SECRETS. San Francisco: Harper and Row.

ACKNOWLEDGMENTS

They say this life comes out of dreamtime and returns to dream-time. When I began collecting the dreams of African-American people and researching the African world that gave birth to black American culture — four years before we met in the flesh — Mandaza visited me in a dream. We were in a small room and he pointed to a presence I could not see in the corner. "She says congratulations, you have made it. It was very hard to get here but you are home."

Likewise, many years before, when Mandaza was being initiated by a medicine man (nganga) of the "enemy" tribe, the Ndebele, he was delivered in a dream to the stony holy land of Matopos in southern Zimbabwe. He wandered the hillsides looking for his white brother.

The first evening we were together he began initiating me into the ngoma of the water spirits. In his little spirit room he started by introducing me to the invisibles with whom he keeps company. Pointing to the corner to the mambokadzi, the mother of the water spirits he said, "She says congratulations, you have made it".

"I wondered when you were going to say that", I responded. When I told him why I was laughing it became clear to him that I was the white brother. "Like you'" he said, "I came to my so-called enemy to be initiated."

It is said we come out of the world of the ancestors and return to the world of the ancestors — true both of this life but also the cycles of initiation that makes one a nganga. At the end of my first initiation I dreamt that the Ndebele ancestors of Mandaza's wife, Simakuhle, were washing my naked body in cool fire. "Now the white man can ripen slowly," intoned a Grandfather.

Finally, it is said that before any ritual gesture—such as offering this book at last to the world — one sings homage to the ancestors and the invisibles, the midzimu.

Praise be to the ancestors of the Ndebele people who came to trust this vagrant soul who wandered into their circle. Praise be to Mandaza's Shona ancestors who still till the soil and raise the maize. Praises to mandlovu, the elephant, who draws strangers into family and Ambuya Bwebwe, Grandmother Spider, who cast the thread that brought me to Zimbabwe. Praises, of course, to the njuzu spirits of healing and peacemaking, the water spirits ancient beyond telling, relentlessly kind in dissolving my stubborn resistance.

Homage to my father, Milford Lee Hill, who dared marry across the fictional borders of race and to my Mexican grandfather, Frank Ortiz, who introduced me to the holiness of water as a farmer and keeper of the acequia.

Homage to all whom have passed before.

I procrastinated for years before I told my mother, Adelina Ortiz de Hill, that I was going to Africa to be initiated. A religious Catholic, she didn't miss a beat: "It's about time. We're always insisting native people go our way." Thanks, Mom.

Gratitude to Kykosa Kajangu who was able to verify my understanding of the Kongo world and the Liberian peacemaker Bill Saa who has taught me so much about how to carry the tradition that has received me.

When I asked AJ (Andrew Johnson), out of South Chicago, "When will black folk stop with the 'what's up with the African thing, white boy?'" he laughed his inimitable laugh.

"Never."

Thank you, AJ, for the reality check.

When I told Tsehai Farrell about this conversation she concurred that I was fortunate for such generosity, such honesty.

"He'd be lying if he said otherwise."

I met Tsehai through her book and workshop, "Transformation of Race", where she looks at the wounds racism has visited on blacks and whites and the ubiquitous "others." Her brilliance, humor and dedication to Spirit are an inspiration. Our dialogues on race have much informed this book.

Gratitude to Musikavanhu and Tsitsi Hougabook, the first African-Americans Mandaza and I were honored to initiate into the Water Spirit tradition. Thank you for making the bridges that Mandaza be received in the African-American world.

Gratitude to my wife, Deena Metzger, her patience and impatience, her wisdom and her Brooklyn humor. Deena of the wild gray hair was accepted as elder and tete (aunt) in Zimbabwe and over the years has tempered and made viable in North America what I learned in Africa.

Thanks to Carol Sheppard who helped refine the final draft and assisted me lovingly in my efforts to bring this out in the world.

Gratitude to Jay Salter, mad enough to live the life of a poet in this day and age, for his refinement of the conclusionary poem. Il miglior fabbro!

Gratitude and again gratitude to the dreamers who made this book possible.

May I do you honor.

ABOUT THE AUTHORS

MICHAEL ORTIZ HILL is an author, registered nurse, and practitioner of traditional African medicine in the United States and among Bantu people in Zimbabwe. Born in 1957 to a Mexican Catholic mother and an Anglo-Buddhist father, his life always involved moving between different cultural communities.

Taught Buddhist meditation by his father as a teenager, Hill ultimately received formal training in the Zen and Vajrayana (Tibetan) Buddhist traditions. He later brought his Buddhist practice to bear on hospice care of people with life-threatening diseases and underwent training as a registered nurse. During this time he practiced as a lay monk and spent a year and a half in complete solitude refining his meditation practice.

In 1996, Hill met the Bantu healer Mandaza Augustine Kandemwa in Africa. Hill became the first non-African initiated into the tradition of the water spirits, and since then Hill and Mandaza have been collaborating in the work of healing, initiation, and understanding the deep African patterning in the dream life and spirit world of African American people. Hill and Mandaza co-founded the Nganga Project, a nonprofit that sustains African healing and makes alliances between healers of different traditions (African, Native American, Western biomedicine). The Nganga Project purchased land in Zimbabwe — a "peace farm" to collectively grow food for the hungry and draw together people from the various races and ethnicities in a country that has been ravaged by intergroup violence. More information can be found on Ortiz Hill's website, gatheringin.com.

MANDAZA AUGUSTINE KANDEMWA is widely recognized in Southern Africa as a traditional healer (nganga). Roughly 60 years old (he doesn't know the year of his birth), Kandemwa's father was poisoned by witches when he was a boy. Very much a child of poverty, he spent his early years living with various relatives, working the fields and, by his own volition, struggling to get whatever education he could in various missionary-run schools. Kandemwa came of age during the resistance to apartheid in his country and as a teenager was involved in clandestine activity. He was trained as a teacher and was recognized as having exceptional skill at organizing schools. In the late sixties, he was recruited against his will into the British South African Police as a teacher and, ultimately, as school administrator.

During his tenure in the police force, Kandemwa was afflicted with severe water spirit disease, understood to be the call of the ancestors to practice as a traditional healer. He was then a staunchly religious Christian and did not heed the call and so suffered years of disorientation even as he rose in the ranks of the police. Eventually he dreamed he was to be initiated by an Ndebele nganga – the Ndebele being the historical enemies of the Shona (Kandemwa's tribe). A few days later, his job transferred him to an Ndebele-speaking part of the country where he was approached by a stranger, a nganga, who ultimately took him through the rites of initiation.

On the eve of his promotion to the highest rank in police school administration in Zimbabwe, he left his job to be a full-time nganga and peacemaker, accepting no fee in working with the poor and working class people of Bulawayo, the country's second largest city.

DR. KYKOSA KAJANGU is a both a scholar of African wisdom traditions and a knowledge-holder of the Bashi people of the Democratic Republic of Congo. Currently, he serves as a visiting professor in the Department of Religion and Philosophy at Southwestern University.